THE 1st BATTALION
DORSETSHIRE REGIMENT
IN FRANCE AND BELGIUM
AUGUST, 1914, TO JUNE, 1915

THE 1st BATTALION
DORSETSHIRE REGIMENT
IN FRANCE AND BELGIUM
AUGUST 1914 TO JUNE 1915

**INCLUDING A ROLL OF OFFICERS, LIST OF HONOURS
AND AWARDS, MENTIONS IN DESPATCHES
AND SUMMARY OF CASUALTIES**

WITH ELEVEN MAPS

The Naval & Military Press Ltd

Published by

The Naval & Military Press Ltd
Unit 10 Ridgewood Industrial Park,
Uckfield, East Sussex,
TN22 5QE England

Tel: +44 (0) 1825 749494
Fax: +44 (0) 1825 765701

www.naval-military-press.com
www.nmarchive.com

CONTENTS

APPENDICES

MAPS

NOTE

THIS short narrative of operations, in which the 1st Battalion Dorsetshire Regiment took part in France and Belgium from August, 1914, to June, 1915, is based upon the official war diary, supplemented by the writer's own recollections. A short account has been added at various points in the narrative of the plans and operations of the enemy in so far as they affect that part of the field upon which the Dorsets were engaged. This it has been possible to do from a study of the official *History of the War*, Volume I, and Von Kluck's *March on Paris.*

It is thought that the period under review is perhaps of some interest, as for several months a war of movement was in progress, and, further, the operations dealt with give some idea of the enormous task which the old Regular Army was called upon to undertake.

It is also hoped that the narrative, which deals with the part played by individual companies, may be of some slight value in providing material from which young soldiers, who join these same companies in the days to come, may learn the great traditions established by their predecessors in the greatest war in history.

Every effort has been made to ensure that the list of honours, awards, and mentions in despatches is correct, but the writer wishes to apologise for any errors or omissions that may have arisen. Owing to the impossibility of obtaining official information the summary of casualties can only be taken as approximately accurate.

A. L. R.

PLYMOUTH,
April, 1923.

THE 1st BATTALION
DORSETSHIRE REGIMENT
IN FRANCE AND BELGIUM

AUGUST, 1914, TO JUNE, 1915

I

MOBILISATION

The 15th Infantry Brigade—Events in Ulster and war rumours—
" Mobilise " — Mobilisation   complete — Embarkation — Havre
reached.

IN the summer of 1914 the 1st Battalion Dorset Regiment
was stationed at Victoria Barracks, Belfast, and formed
part of the 15th Infantry Brigade, under command of
Brig.-Gen. Count Gleichen (now Major-Gen. Lord Edward
Gleichen, K.C.V.O., C.B., C.M.G., D.S.O.).   The remaining battalions of the brigade were 1st Bn. Norfolk
Regiment (Holywood), 1st Bn. Bedfordshire Regiment
(Mullingar), and 1st Bn. Cheshire Regiment (London-
derry).   The 15th Infantry Brigade belonged to the
5th Division, commanded by Major-Gen. Sir Charles
Fergusson, Bart., C.B., M.V.O., D.S.O., the remaining
brigades of which were the 13th, stationed at Dublin,
and the 14th at the Curragh.

The spring and early summer of 1914 had been a time
of considerable unrest in the north of Ireland, and for
several months the thoughts of all had been turned
towards the possibility of civil war in Ulster.   So the
events on the Continent in July, following upon the
assassination of the heir to the throne of Austria at
Serajevo at the end of June, did not perhaps make the
same impression upon the minds of the army in Ireland
as might otherwise have been the case, and the sudden
call to arms in a much greater adventure than civil
strife in Ulster could have entailed came in the nature
of a surprise.

But, nevertheless, the possibilities of a European war were being eagerly discussed during the last week in July, and just when it was felt that the crisis might pass, orders suddenly arrived one evening that the instructions for what was officially termed the " Precautionary Period " were to be put into practice.

These instructions, which were a necessary prelude to mobilisation, provided for the protection of a number of " vulnerable points " in the neighbourhood of Belfast—forts on the coast, waterworks, cable lines, etc.—and protective detachments were always kept in readiness for the purpose. These detachments were despatched early the following morning.

Events on the Continent were moving rapidly, but for days the policy of the British Government was unknown to the general public. By the 3rd August (Bank Holiday) Great Britain was on the verge of war. The order to mobilise was expected at any moment. On the afternoon of the 4th it reached the battalion, the message reading : " Mobilise. To-morrow, 5th August, is the 1st day of mobilisation." (Timed 5.39 p.m.)

From the moment of the receipt of this order, the long prepared and carefully rehearsed scheme of mobilisation was put into practice. Two officers (Lieut. Pitt, the Assistant-Adjutant, and 2/Lieut. Chapman) and 3 N.C.O.'s left Belfast the same night for Dorchester to conduct Reservists and took with them the Colours of the battalion. Two further detachments were despatched to garrison " vulnerable points."

Wednesday, the 5th of August (first day of mobilisa-tion), saw the mobilisation scheme in full swing. All ranks were medically inspected, and the men under age and medically unfit (there were very few of the latter) were handed over to the " Details," now under temporary command of Capt. Hyslop.

An important telegram arrived from the War Office late in the day to the effect that men between the ages of nineteen and twenty years, who had fired Table A, were to proceed overseas with the battalion. This order caused some difficulty, as the bulk of the men affected had been included among the various detachments sent away to guard vulnerable points, because under the existing regulations they were too young to proceed overseas ; their mobilisation preparation was consequently delayed until they could be relieved by Special Reserve units.

The following appointments were made : Staff-Capt., 15th Infantry Brigade, Capt. A. L. Moulton-Barrett ; Battalion Transport Officer : Lieut. C. F. M. Margetts.

Thursday, 6th August (second day of mobilisation), saw the arrival of a party of 5 officers (Capts. Kitchin and Roe, Lieuts. Turner and Burnand, 3rd Battalion, and 2/Lieut. Shannon, Supplementary List), and 96 Reservists, who arrived from Dorchester, via Heysham. Capt. Kitchin at once assumed command of the Details, vice Capt. Hyslop, who proceeded to France in advance of the battalion on special duty and rejoined it in the concentration area later.

The following postings were made :

" A " Company : Lieut. F. D. S. King, 2/Lieut. G. S. Shannon.

" B " Company : Lieut. J. R. Turner.

" C " Company : Lieut. G. A. Burnand.

The following were attached to the Details : Capt. A. R. M. Roe (later posted to " B " Company, and for a short period Brigade Machine-Gun Officer) ; Capt. W. F. G. Willes, 2nd Battalion ; Capt. A. B. Priestley.

On Friday, 7th August, a second party of Reservists arrived by rail, having crossed via Holyhead and Dublin —strength 5 officers (Lieuts. Pitt, Clarke, Gregory, and Clutterbuck, and 2/Lieut. Price) and 440 Reservists. This was a very fine party, and the appearance of the men made a great impression as they marched through the streets to Victoria Barracks.

On Saturday, 8th August, four detachments returned on relief from " vulnerable points," and were medically inspected and equipped. It is worthy of note that on this day a party of 3 officers (Capt. Willes and Lieuts. Clarke and Gregory) and 14 N.C.O.'s were despatched to Dorchester to act as instructors for a new unit which the War Office was about to raise. Thus were born the divisions of the New or Kitchener's Army, which largely bore the brunt of the war in later years. The unit for which Capt. Willes' party was destined was afterwards known as the 5th Bn. Dorset Regiment and was raised and commanded by Major C. C. Hannay (now Brig.-Gen. Hannay, D.S.O.), then commanding the depot at Dorchester. The 5th Dorsets afterwards formed part of the 11th Division and fought with distinction at Suvla Bay and later in France and Belgium.

During the afternoon of this day there arrived a further party from Dorchester under Lieut. T. H. Clemson, 3rd Battalion, strength 27 N.C.O.'s and men of the regular establishment of the depot, and 32 Reservists.

The following appointments were made : Battalion Machine-Gun Officer : Lieut. C. H. Woodhouse. O.C. First Reinforcement : Capt. A. B. Priestley.

The Battalion Machine-Gun Officer—Lieut. W. B. Algeo—had been seriously ill during the summer, and was unfit for service on mobilisation. He had done much to bring the efficiency of his section to the high standard which it maintained until it was practically wiped out in May, 1915. Lieut. Algeo afterwards commanded " B " Company in 1915 and 1916 and gained the Military Cross. He was killed in a daylight patrol near Thiepval in May, 1916—a great loss to the regiment.

By Sunday, 9th August, the battalion was up to war strength in numbers (about fifty per cent being Reservists) and equipment, and orders for embarkation were awaited. The mobilisation process had worked with remarkable smoothness which reflected great credit on all concerned, and particularly upon Capt. G. H. Gyngell, the Quartermaster, on whom the bulk of the work of preparation had fallen. It was hard indeed upon Capt. Gyngell that he should have been found medically unfit to proceed overseas. His place was taken by Major J. Kearney, the Quartermaster of the 3rd Battalion.

As the days passed, and no orders for embarkation arrived, doubts began to fill the minds of all as to whether, after all, the battalion was to proceed to France. It was not until Wednesday, 12th August, that orders did reach the battalion. It is understood that they had been held back at Brigade Headquarters since the 8th in compliance with instructions from Higher Authority.

But the days of waiting were not wasted ; indeed, they were of the greatest value in many ways. Men settled down in their sections and platoons, various necessary inspections were held, boots were fitted, and hundreds of other details attended to. Training was carried out at Cave Hill and vicinity daily, culminating on the 12th in a battalion field firing exercise. This training and the necessary marches to and from the training ground were of inestimable value, as future events substantially proved.

Early on Friday, 14th August, the embarkation of the battalion on s.s. *Anthony* commenced. The embarkation of the horses—no easy task—was admirably carried out under the direction of the Transport Officer (Lieut. Margetts), and was completed by 1.30 p.m. The personnel of the battalion then embarked. Headquarters 15th Infantry Brigade and 1st Norfolk Regiment (less two companies) were also on board.

s.s. *Anthony* sailed at 3.25 p.m. and proceeded slowly down Belfast Lough, whilst crowds on both banks gave their friends a great send-off. How many at that time realised what an European war meant ! The voyage was uneventful. The weather was fine and hot, and the sea smooth. Havre was reached at 4 p.m. on Sunday, 16th August, and the disembarkation commenced at once.

At 8 p.m. the Dorsets set out through Havre to No. 8 Rest Camp some miles beyond the town, and on the top of a big hill, the march occupying two hours. The streets of the town were lined by large and enthusiastic crowds who lavished large quantities of flowers upon the troops, exacting in return souvenirs in the shape of cap and shoulder badges. Owing to the steepness of the approach to the camp, the transport had to be left behind, and all ranks passed a somewhat uncomfortable night, the camp site being very wet.

II

CONCENTRATION

Entrainment—Detrainment at Le Cateau—Billets at Ors—
Concentration area of B.E.F.

At 8 p.m. on 17th August the Dorsets began to entrain at Havre for an unknown destination and departed at 11 p.m. The entrainment of the vehicles was particularly well carried out by " C " Company, assisted by two sections of " B " Company. The Railway Transport Officer stated that the time taken was the best by ten minutes of any unit so far entrained.

At 2.20 p.m. on the 18th August Busigny was reached, where orders were received that the train was to proceed to Le Cateau which was reached at 3.20 p.m. The detraining of the vehicles was well carried out by two platoons of " D " Company, and the Dorsets moved by march route to Ors, a small village on the Sambre Canal, where they went into billets. This was a lengthy process in the light of subsequent experience, but was at last completed, taking about three hours in all, with all ranks comfortably settled down. Late that night an order to place posts at two points north of the village to guard against a possible advance of hostile cavalry brought home the fact that at last the battalion was on active service.

For the two following days the Dorsets remained at Ors, while the IInd Corps (3rd and 5th Divisions) was in process of concentration. On the 20th August the Dorsets were addressed by Major-Gen. Sir Charles Fergusson, G.O.C. 5th Division (to which the 15th Brigade belonged), and a warning order was received that a forward movement was to begin on the following day.[1]

[1] The British Expeditionary Force concentrated in the area west of Maubeuge. It consisted of the Ist Corps (1st and 2nd Divisions) and the IInd Corps (3rd and 5th Divisions).

The 5th Division concentrated in the area Le Cateau–Landrecies, with the 3rd Division to the north-east of it. The 19th Infantry Brigade (made up of battalions destined originally for the Lines of Communication) was railed up to Valenciennes on 22nd August and marched on 23rd to Condé, linking up with the left of the 5th Division along the Mons–Condé Canal.

The 4th Division began to arrive at Le Cateau on 25th and, coming under orders of the G.O.C. IInd Corps, took part in the battle of Le Cateau on 26th on the left of the British line.

14

III

ADVANCE TO THE MONS–CONDÉ CANAL

(See Map X)

The advance begins—Absence of information—Intense heat—
Billets at Dour.

AT 4 a.m. on 21st August the 15th Brigade began its
march northwards, the Dorsets being the Advanced
Guard. The route lay via Englefontaine–Potelle to
Gommegnies, where the Dorsets halted with " C," " A,"
and " B " Companies finding outposts on the line Le
Cheval Blanc–Preux. The outpost companies were
relieved later by units of the 14th Brigade, and the
Dorsets went into billets at Gommegnies. The distance
marched was nineteen miles in fine and hot weather.

It would be well to say here that at this time only the
vaguest information was available in the battalion as
regards the enemy. Except that it had been stated
that contact with him might be expected by the following
Sunday afternoon (23rd August)—a prediction which
turned out to be extraordinarily correct—nothing else
was known. And this state of affairs continued throughout the early stages of the fighting, so that all ranks grew
to understand fully what historians meant when they
wrote of the " Fog of War."

Next morning, 22nd August, saw a very early start
(3.30 a.m.), and some confusion and delay at the starting-
point, caused by the hour of starting being advanced at
short notice. It was a very hot morning, and the march
proved particularly trying to the Reservists. The route
lay via Bavai–Houdain–Athis to Dour. As soon as the
frontier had been crossed, and the column had entered
Belgium, the general aspect of the countryside underwent
a marked change. This district, the south-western outskirts of the Mons–Charleroi mining area, was industrial,
and its villages much more densely populated than those
on the French side of the frontier. For the first time
roads paved with cobble stones, very uneven and trying
to the feet, were met with. The inhabitants from out-
ward appearances gave the impression of being less

friendly than the French peasants. They watched the passage of the troops through their midst with marked indifference. Men of military age were numerous in the villages, lounging at street corners as the troops passed.

This industrial area, prolific in man-power, should serve as a warning to this country. When later the Germans occupied the district, the population was conscripted, and the men—and sometimes even the women—were deported to Germany, and elsewhere, for forced labour.

The Dorsets went into billets at Dour, the remainder of the brigade being at Bois de Boussu. The distance marched on this day was fifteen miles.

IV

THE BATTLE OF MONS

(SEE MAPS A AND X)

Occupation of the Wasmes position—First contact with the enemy—
Dispositions at nightfall 23rd August, 1914—Surprise orders—
The battle renewed—Capt. Williams' fine stand at Wasmes—
First Line Transport ambushed—Lieut. Margetts wins the D.S.O.
—The Great Retreat begins—Bivouac at St. Vaast—German
plans and operations in the battle—Casualties.

NOTHING occurred to disturb the battalion on Sunday
morning, 23rd August, though along the Mons–Condé
Canal, where the 13th and 14th Brigades were in position
with outposts on the north bank, heavy German attacks
began to develop during the morning and early afternoon.

About 12 noon, orders arrived that half-battalions of
the brigade were to proceed at once to a position running
from Wasmes along the railway to Boussu, there to
entrench. Accordingly Battalion Headquarters, with
" C " and " D " Companies, marched via Bois de Boussu
and thence along the railway to a railway bridge on the
northern outskirts of Wasmes where the railway crosses
the road to Wasmuel. The country in this neighbourhood was extremely enclosed, consisting of narrow
streets, gardens, slag heaps, factories, and railway works.
However, " C " Company were ordered to entrench on a
small hill about 500 yards north-west of the railway
bridge where the ground afforded a good field of fire,
facing north and north-east, with a company of the
Bedfords on their right lining the railway; " D "
Company for the time being were held in reserve. On
" C " Company's left was a gap, for the front allotted
was too great to be held continuously, and then came
the Cheshires, who were digging in south of Hornu.
Later, " D " Company was ordered to entrench on the
right of the Bedfords.

Heavy fighting was now going on along the Canal
at Mariette and St. Ghislain and numerous shell-bursts
could be observed, but the 15th Brigade was for the time
being unmolested. About 4 p.m. a message was received
that the 3rd Division (on right of the 5th Division) was

retiring to a position south of Mons, and that the 15th
Brigade was to block the Mariette–Paturages Road. In
order to fill the gap caused by the withdrawal of 3rd
Division the Bedfords took up a line from the north-east
of Paturages towards Wasmes.

At 5 p.m. hostile shells began to pass over the Dorsets'
trenches from a north-easterly direction, being directed
chiefly upon the northern outskirts of Wasmes, but they
caused the Dorsets no casualties.

At 5.30 p.m. about a battalion of infantry was
observed halted in a cornfield about 1000 yards north-
east of " D " Company's trenches. Col. Bols refused at
first to allow any fire to be opened as he was uncertain
whether they were hostile troops.[1] But, ignorant of the
order, Lieut. Hawkins' platoon of " D " Company
opened a burst of rapid fire, and these troops hurriedly
took cover.   Gradually small groups of Germans could
be observed approaching the front of the Bedfords and
Dorsets, and about 7.30 p.m. the street just south of the
railway bridge by Battalion Headquarters was heavily
shelled ; but no casualties were suffered. As darkness
fell the firing died away, and at 8.30 p.m. " A " and
" B " Companies and machine-gun section, all under
Major Roper, arrived at the railway bridge.   " A "
Company was sent at once to prolong the left of " C "
Company, in order to fill up the gap existing between
the Dorsets and Cheshires. Two platoons of this company were later withdrawn to Battalion Headquarters,
which passed the night in a street possessing the ominous
name of the Rue des Morts.

The night was very quiet, and about 2 a.m., 24th
August, orders were received that a general retirement
was contemplated, and that the Dorsets were to withdraw to Paturages as soon as relieved by a unit of the
13th Brigade.   These orders gave the first indication
that the general situation was unfavourable to the
Allies. As a gap still existed between the Dorsets and
Cheshires, " B " Company (Capt. Williams) was ordered
to prolong the left of " A " Company and gain touch
with the Cheshires about Hornu. As soon as it was light
the battle was renewed by the guns of both sides. The
enemy could be seen moving in groups and climbing to

---

[1] They were undoubtedly Germans who had followed up the
retiring 3rd Division.

the top of slag heaps to the north-east and east of the Dorsets' trenches, from which commanding positions he soon opened a heavy fire with machine-guns.

At dawn the Dorsets were disposed as follows from right to left : " D " Company (Capt. Davidson) facing north-east ; " C " Company (Major Saunders) holding a small hill and cottage and facing generally north and north-east ; " A " Company (less two platoons) (Capt. Fraser) and " B " Company both facing north. Battalion Headquarters, machine-gun section, and two platoons of " A " Company were at the railway bridge. With the Dorsets was a section of the 17th Field Company R.E. under Lieut. Smyth.

At 4.30 a.m. a message was received at Battalion Headquarters from Capt. Williams (timed 4 a.m.) stating that he was at the railway bridge three-quarters of a mile south-east of Hornu, in touch with " A " Company on his right, but not in touch with the Cheshires. About 6 a.m. " D " Company was relieved by a company of the 2nd Duke of Wellingtons, in accordance with orders, and withdrew to the railway bridge, where Battalion Headquarters were established.

The enemy had now begun to shell heavily the cottage on " C " Company's front and some casualties were caused, probably the first the Dorsets suffered in the Great War. Experienced for the first time the rain of high-explosive shells from the German field howitzers was most disconcerting. The shells burst with an earsplitting crash and threw up clouds of earth. " C " Company's front was soon enshrouded in thick black smoke.

This bombardment rendered the relief by the 2nd Duke of Wellingtons a matter of some difficulty, and when it did take place " C " Company and " A " Company (less two platoons) withdrew to the position held by " B " Company, instead of rejoining as ordered at the railway bridge, the road to which being now exposed to heavy machine-gun fire. This movement might have led to some confusion, for " A " and " C " Companies were somewhat mixed up and without definite orders to meet this suddenly arising situation. In the emergency Capt. Hyslop, the senior officer on the spot, at once took charge and skilfully organised a defensive line in conjunction with Capt. Williams' Company, then in position south-east of Hornu. All accounts agree to the coolness

displayed by Capt. Hyslop at this juncture. Realising
that the men were exposed for the first time to the heavy
machine-gun fire of modern warfare, he scorned to take
cover, moving from place to place over the open as he
organised and encouraged his men. He was soon struck
down and severely wounded, but his gallantry had
achieved its object ; a well-organised line confronted the
enemy, who were by this time swarming over the canal.

Capt. Hyslop was too badly wounded to be moved far
and had the misfortune to fall into German hands.
After his return from Germany he was awarded the
French Croix-de-Guerre as some slight reward for his
gallantry and able leadership on this occasion.

Major Saunders with one platoon of " C " Company
did however rejoin Battalion Headquarters at the
railway bridge, moving under cover of the streets on the
north-western edge of Wasmes.

It is worthy of note that a belated message reached
Battalion Headquarters from Capt. Williams, timed as
late as 11.20 a.m., and is here given in full :

"Am holding my own with 'A,' 'B,' and 'C'
Companies in so far that the enemy cannot get closer
than 200 yards on my right, and 500 yards on my left.
But I am being gradually driven in, and my ammunition is almost exhausted. A counter-attack by some
other unit might save the situation. I have no communication with my right, left, or rear."

The following narrative was supplied by 2/Lieut.
Turner, one of " B " Company's subalterns :

" 'B' Company moved into a railway cutting by a
bridge 600 yards W.N.W. of W. of Wasmes. Two
platoons were pushed forward to entrench. About
6 a.m. the whole company went into the trenches,
having part of 'A' Company on their right and part
of 'C' Company on their left. The enemy's infantry
advanced, supported by heavy artillery fire, but were
repulsed. A lull of one hour followed. The enemy then
opened a heavy rifle and artillery fire. It was seen
that the enemy had worked round both flanks. About
2 p.m. the company was ordered to retire, and fell
back in the direction of Blaugies. Capt. Williams
with about a dozen men covered the retirement of the
remainder."

This party became detached from the battalion and actually fought two days later with a unit of the 14th Brigade.

About 8 a.m. Battalion Headquarters, two platoons " A " Company, " D " Company, and the machine-gun section moved through the streets to their rendezvous at Paturages, where Brigade Headquarters was already established. The 1st Line Transport, under Lieut. Margetts, had already reached this point. Two platoons of " A " Company, under Lieut. Pitt, were at once sent to support the Bedfords who held a position on the north-eastern edge of the town.

As it was obvious that the enemy had penetrated a considerable distance on the east, a further retirement was contemplated. Accordingly Brig.-Gen. Count Gleichen directed Lieut. Margetts to move off the 1st Line Transport of Brigade Headquarters and of the Dorsets at once and, in order to avoid the steep hill through Petit Wasmes, selected a more southerly and apparently safe road via La Bouverie. The column of transport had not proceeded far, however, when it encountered a battalion of Germans [1] which had encircled Paturages and had apparently entered it from the south-east. The Germans opened heavy rifle fire upon the transport, and several horses were hit. Lieut. Margetts thereupon rode forward and engaged the attention of the Germans with his revolver, while the transport column turned about and withdrew. In doing so he was badly wounded, and, as he could not be moved, he had to be left in a house and was later taken prisoner. By his personal gallantry and presence of mind he undoubtedly saved the whole column. He was later awarded the D.S.O., the first gained by an officer of the regiment in the Great War.

As it was now clear that the enemy was closing in on Paturages, and as the town was now being shelled from three directions, the Dorsets withdrew slowly, and unmolested by hostile infantry, via Petit Wasmes–Warquignies to Blaugies, while the Bedfords fell back by a more southerly road. Paturages was full of inhabitants who, unmindful of the shells, stood in the doorways of their houses and offered wine and water to the troops. This retirement began about 11 a.m., and was slow and

[1] Part of the 20th Regiment of the 6th German Division.

tiring in the intense heat, and on the steep and cobbled streets. After Warquignies the country opened out and Blaugies was reached without further incident.[1]

At Blaugies, the remainder of the Dorsets, viz. two platoons of " A " Company, " B " Company, and " C " Company, gradually rejoined after their stubborn fight north-west of Wasmes. About 4 p.m. the retirement was continued via Athis to St. Waast where the 15th Brigade bivouacked. Thus ended the Battle of Mons as far as the Dorsets were concerned.

The 24th August was a day of confused fighting, complicated by uncertainty as regards the flanks, lack of training in street fighting, and embarrassment over the crowds of civilians thronging the streets. The enemy was well supplied with artillery and machine-guns, added to which his superior numbers enabled him to push through the many gaps in our line under cover of the numerous avenues of approach which this industrial area afforded.

It is interesting to follow the operations of the German Corps operating on the front St. Ghislain–Jemappes as it is now possible to do from a study of recently published books and articles.[2]

On 23rd August the IIIrd German Corps had orders to march, its 5th Division to St. Ghislain, its 6th Division to the high ground south of Jemappes.

Operations of the 5th Division, IIIrd Corps.

All attempts to force a crossing of the canal at St. Ghislain failed with heavy loss. The German Regiment attacking this front, 12th Grenadiers, lost 25 officers and 500 other ranks killed and wounded, and its moral was considerably shaken by its failure, as the German account frankly admits.

After several failures the 3/8th Grenadiers captured the bridge at Mariette, at the boundary between the British 3rd and 5th Divisions, solely by means of a section of guns brought up to very close range. By 5 p.m. the 8th Grenadiers were in possession of Mariette. In order to assist in the attack on St. Ghislain, the 1/8th Grenadiers turned west and approached Hornu ; meanwhile

---

[1] The 54th Regiment had hastened along this same route to the assault of Cambrai on the 24th June, 1815, when advanced guard to Colville's Division of Wellington's Army.

[2] *March on Paris*, Von Kluck, and " The Battle of Mons," published in the *Journal* of the Royal United Service Institution, August, 1921.

the 2/8th and 3/8th Grenadiers turned towards Wasmuel, which they occupied at 8 p.m. Darkness prevented further progress.

Operations of the 6th Division, IIIrd Corps.

After heavy fighting the 1/24th Regiment captured the bridge at Jemappes and occupied the town. The 64th Regiment followed, and later the 2/24th and 3/24th. By the evening these regiments were concentrated on the high ground south of Jemappes. The 6th Division was intended to occupy the high ground at Frameries on this day, and towards 8 p.m. the advance was resumed. But in the gathering darkness direction could not be maintained in a country of a very enclosed nature, and the movement was given up. The 6th Division settled down for the night on the general line of the railway Quaregnon–Flenu and east of the latter place, covered by battle outposts. Elements of this division were seen and fired on by "D" Company of the Dorsets as already related.

The plan of the commander of the IIIrd German Corps for 24th August was as follows :

The 5th Division, after capturing St. Ghislain (which it had failed to do on the 23rd), was to place itself south of Hornu ready to operate in a south-westerly direction.

The 6th Division was to be on the high ground at Frameries at 4 a.m., ready to continue the advance.

Operations of the 5th Division, IIIrd Corps.

The 1/52nd and 2/52nd Regiment, after crossing the canal at points seized during the night, moved towards Boussu and Hornu about 5 a.m., supported by the 48th Regiment.

The 12th Grenadiers occupied St. Ghislain, the canal bridges having been given up by the British during the night according to plan. But the 52nd and 48th Regiments became heavily engaged south of Hornu, while the 8th Grenadiers, advancing east of Hornu, encountered British troops holding a position north and north-west of Wasmes. This latter position was the one already described as occupied by the Dorsets under Capt. Williams. The Germans here appear, from their own accounts, to have suffered a serious check, for it was not until 2.25 p.m. that the situation was clear enough for the commander of the 5th German Division to issue orders for a further attack. Even then it is stated that the attack did not make proper headway until supported by artillery which was brought over the canal with great difficulty. The account goes on to state that the enemy abandoned his positions at 3 p.m. and retired south, procedure justified both by superior orders and by normal rearguard tactics.

Operations of the 6th Division, IIIrd Corps.

At dawn the whole of the artillery of the 6th Division opened a heavy fire on Frameries and the vicinity.

The German account states that events of the 23rd had shown that, without a heavy preliminary bombardment by artillery, village and house-to-house fighting involved unduly high casualties. The attack began at 8.30 a.m., the 20th Regiment being directed on Paturages, the 12th Brigade on Frameries. The Germans encountered, according to their own accounts, a desperate resistance, but by 12 noon they had reached the main Paturages–Frameries Road. At the same time the 20th Regiment penetrated into Paturages, and it must have been troops of this regiment who so narrowly missed capturing the Dorsets' transport. The British troops then fell back, in accordance with orders, the Germans losing touch with them, for the account then goes on to state that new orders were issued for the 5th Division from Hornu to advance towards Warquignies, the 6th Division to support it moving south of Paturages. No further fighting took place, and as early as 6 p.m. the 3rd German Corps halted for the night, the 5th Division in and north of Dour, the 6th Division in and north of Warquignies. Thus the Germans lost touch with the British rearguards.

The casualties of the Dorsets for this day were as follows :

Officers.—Wounded and taken prisoner : Capt. R. G. B. M. Hyslop, Lieut. C. F. M. Margetts, Lieut. W. A. Leishman. Missing : Capt. H. S. Williams,[1] Lieut. G. A. Burnand.[1]

Other ranks.—Killed, 12 ; wounded, 49 ; missing, 69.

It is worthy of note that the average distance marched on 24th August, exclusive of fighting, was fifteen miles.

[1] Afterwards rejoined 5th Division at Le Cateau and fought with 2nd Suffolk Regiment on 26th August, Capt. Williams being wounded and Lieut. Burnand taken prisoner on that date.

V

THE RETIREMENT TO AND BATTLE ON THE LE CATEAU POSITION

(SEE MAP B)

A trying march—The Dorsets reach Troisvilles—The decision to stand and fight—Dispositions 6 a.m.—The course of the battle—The battle broken off—The Dorsets' disciplined withdrawal—The halt at Ponchaux—German operations on 26th August, 1914.

THE 15th Brigade continued its retirement at 2 a.m. on 25th August, marching via Bavai–Englefontaine–Le Cateau. The early start prevented the issue of supplies to the troops. The supplies had been dumped at a certain point, but there was no time to collect them. There followed a very trying march. By 9 a.m. the sun had grown exceedingly hot, which, added to the absence of breakfast, was a severe trial to the troops after the heavy work of the past few days. The road, which traversed for the greater part of its length the north-western edge of Mormal Forest, perfectly straight for miles, seemed endless to the weary troops. It was crowded with inhabitants hurrying south-westwards, carrying bundles, and wheeling their belongings in carts and barrows. The effect was depressing and brought home only too clearly what retreat entailed. An hour's halt at Englefontaine, and the collection of such supplies as could be obtained were very welcome. German aeroplanes now began to hover overhead, watching the progress of the column, and did so unmolested. At that time there was an order forbidding fire to be opened on any aeroplane. The Dorsets passed through Le Cateau, at which place they had detrained only a week previously, and went into bivouac about 2 p.m. on the open downs one mile east of Troisvilles. Some trenches had been dug south of the Le Cateau–Cambrai Road by inhabitants, and Lieut.-Col. Bols and the company commanders reconnoitred these at once. " A " Company was thereupon placed on outpost near the road junction half-mile N.E. of La Sotiere, a hamlet really forming part of the village of Troisvilles.

The remainder of the Dorsets remained in bivouac,

Supplies arrived and were distributed, and the men set to work to make themselves comfortable, using the numerous corn stooks for the purpose. Reconnaissances by hostile aircraft continued during the evening, which turned wet. During the afternoon masses of French cavalry crossed the downs, moving generally westward.[1]

About 1 a.m. on 26th August the Dorsets were ordered to stand to arms at once, as some outpost troops of another battalion had fallen back. Companies fell in quietly and without confusion in the darkness in an altogether admirable manner. All being quiet, the troops were allowed to fall out once more.

An order had been received that the brigade was to continue its retirement at 7 a.m. on 26th August to Estrees. But this order was cancelled about 4 a.m.

Into the reasons which caused the commander of the IInd Corps to fight on the Le Cateau position it is impossible to enter in this narrative. To the troops on the spot at the time there seemed nothing surprising in the order to occupy the trenches along the ridge between Le Cateau and Troisvilles, which had been reconnoitred the previous day. This was done at 5 a.m., and the battalion was disposed as follows :

Two platoons of " C " Company under Lieut. Fraser held an advanced position south of the Le Cateau–Cambrai Road in touch with the Bedfords on their right. The remainder of " C " Company dug themselves in the northern edge of La Sotiere, and Lieut. Woodhouse placed his machine-guns close to this point where they could sweep the approaches to the village. " B " Company (now under Capt. Roe), on the left, held the northern edge of Troisvilles, overlooking the valley which runs thence down to Inchy. Further to their left the 9th Brigade (3rd Division) were entrenching lower down the slope towards Inchy. " D " Company set to work to dig in with their " grubbers " on the open ground east of La Sotiere, while "A" Company occupied some orchards between La Sotiere and Troisvilles. Battalion Headquarters were established in a cottage at the road junction on the northern edge of La Sotiere in " C " Company's area which Major Saunders set about strengthening by all available means.

Le Cateau was largely an artillery battle, and from the

[1] Gen. Sordet's Cavalry Corps.

nature of the German plan to press back and envelop both flanks of the IInd Corps, the weight of the attack did not fall upon the Dorsets who were in the centre of the British line. But hostile attacks upon the 13th and 14th Brigades on the right and upon the 9th Brigade on the left could be seen from the battalion front. About 11 a.m. the 9th Brigade had repulsed a strong attack, and the hostile fire having slackened somewhat on that part of the front, Lieut.-Col. Bols, considering the situation to be favourable, asked permission about noon to counter-attack towards Inchy, in conjunction with the 9th Brigade, but his request was not acceded to. About 1 p.m. intense rifle fire could be heard on the right, where the Germans were closing in on the right flank of the 14th Brigade, but the battalion front remained quiet, and Troisvilles itself had not been shelled, most of the hostile fire being directed at our artillery positions, many of which were in the open and quite visible. About 2 p.m. our troops could be seen falling back on our right on the front of other brigades, and heavy fire continued to be heard from that direction, but the line of the 15th Brigade was still intact, and no organised attack had yet developed against it. At 3.10 p.m. a message was received from the 15th Brigade, timed 2.50 p.m., to the effect that the right of the 5th Division was falling back, and that, if obliged to do so, the Dorsets were to retire slowly at once in a S.S.W. direction, via Bertry–Maretz–Estrees, covering their own retirement. As the front of the Dorsets was still in no way pressed, Lieut.-Col. Bols decided to hold on, but he directed the 1st Line Transport, now under Lieut. Partridge, to retire at once. But now the enemy began to grow more enterprising and to push forward machine-guns, but he was held by the Dorsets' machine-gun section under Lieut. Woodhouse, which did splendid work at this period. Lieut.-Col. Bols, being unable to get touch with any other troops on the flanks, had at about 4 p.m. directed " B " Company (Capt. Roe) to take up a covering position about half-mile in rear.

As the enemy had begun to shell the battalion front and was ranging on Troisvilles about this period, Lieut.-Col. Bols, finding the Dorsets isolated, gave orders for a general retirement, which took place at 4.20 p.m., covered by " B " Company. The retirement was admirably carried out under heavy shrapnel fire via Bertry and

Maretz. It was a slow and tedious business, for the road
was blocked by transport and stragglers. Night came on
and a drizzling rain began to fall, but still the march
continued. Estrees was the destination, but owing to
the delay on the road and to the fatigue of the troops,
Lieut.-Col. Bols decided to halt at Ponchaux, a small
village on the Maretz–Estrees Road, and the whole
battalion occupied a sugar factory in the village about
11 p.m. The men were dog tired and went to sleep at
once, uncertain whether any friendly troops lay between
them and the pursuing Germans. It is now known that
the enemy was so exhausted by his long marches, and
had suffered so heavily from the efficiency of British
rifle fire, that he was for the time being incapable of an
energetic pursuit.

The German accounts of the battle of Le Cateau are
meagre. Von Kluck, the Commander of the First
German Army, was labouring under a misapprehension ;
he supposed that the British Army was based on the
Channel ports, and that its line of communication ran in
a westerly direction. His orders for the 26th August
were therefore based on the supposition that the British
front faced east ; it, in fact, faced approximately north.
By the evening of the 25th August the IVth German
Corps had reached the general line Solesmes (6 miles
north of Troisvilles)–Landrecies ; on its left was the IIIrd
Corps about Mormal Forest. These Corps had orders to
march on the 26th August, the IVth Corps to Vendeuille,
the IIIrd Corps to Maretz, distances of 18 miles for the
former and 16 miles for the latter. The rôle of the IIIrd
Corps was one of envelopment of the supposed southern
flank of the British Army.

Directed against Troisvilles and therefore the Dorsets'
main opponent was the 36th Fusilier Regiment of the
15th Infantry Brigade which formed part of the 8th
Division of the IVth Corps. A gap appears to have
existed between this 8th Division and its right-hand
neighbour, the 7th Division, and this may go far to show
why the infantry attack on Troisvilles was not pressed
until the afternoon. The German accounts state that the
attack on the high ground west of Le Cateau began at
11 a.m., but our accounts time it somewhat earlier. As
has already been narrated, the Dorsets' front was not at
any time seriously threatened up to 3.30 p.m. Distant

columns, consisting presumably of the 36th Fusilier Regiment, were observed during the forenoon advancing across the stubble fields towards Inchy, and these were shelled by our guns. By noon small parties had dribbled up to the Le Cateau–Cambrai Road, where they tried to bring machine-guns into position. These were promptly engaged and silenced by Lieut. Woodhouse's guns. There was little or no rifle fire.

Writing of the attack of the IVth Corps, Von Kluck, in his *March on Paris*, says : " The IVth Corps engaged strong forces on the front Caudry–Troisvilles–Reumont at 9 a.m. and got into a difficult position against a well-entrenched enemy." In point of fact the trenches were of a most hasty description, some dug by civilians with farm tools, others by the troops with the small entrenching tool ; all picks and shovels had been left on the field at Mons. It was British rifle fire that produced the " difficult position." As the day advanced the Germans undoubtedly brought an increasing number of guns into action, for the morning's fighting provided a further lesson, after their severe one at Mons, of the futility of coming to close quarters with British riflemen until the latter had been well pounded by artillery.

In considering the day's fighting it is worth while to bear in mind that the 36th Fusilier Regiment, whose objective included Troisvilles, was composed of three battalions and a machine-gun company, and had probably attached to it one Jäger battalion and a Field Artillery Regiment of 24 guns.

The IVth German Corps had by nightfall reached Troisvilles, the IIIrd Corps Reumont, with advanced troops at Honnechy ; that is to say, 12 miles and 3 miles short of their objectives respectively.

The Dorsets' casualties on this day were 14 wounded, 21 missing.

These casualties were very light in comparison with those incurred by many units of the 5th Division, but it must be borne in mind that, while the Dorsets were lucky in not being directly attacked, they were the last battalion of the division to retire from the battle line, and that the retirement was so admirably carried out, and the leadership and discipline so good, that casualties were minimised. If the situation had not been well handled by the commanders of platoons and sections under heavy artillery fire, the casualties would have been numerous. A sudden and powerful burst of fire by two strong companies and two machine-guns, shortly before the withdrawal from Troisvilles commenced, so shook the moral of the attackers lining the Le Cateau–Cambrai Road, and in the stubble fields north-east of it, that their rifle fire became wild and consequently inaccurate.

VI

THE RETREAT ON PARIS

(SEE MAP X)

Retreat of the IInd Corps—Its effect on moral—Value of march discipline—St. Quentin reached—A further effort demanded—Across the Somme—Sir John French inspects the troops on the march—A day's rest at Pontoise—Further rearward marches—In touch with the enemy—The Marne crossed—End of the Great Retreat.

WHAT is now generally known as the "Retreat from Mons" had commenced in earnest. After their short halt at Ponchaux the Dorsets continued the retreat at 3 a.m. on the 27th August towards Estrees. The men were still very tired after an uncomfortable night crowded together and marched on empty stomachs, all supplies having been dumped at Estrees the previous evening. A halt of one hour took place at the latter village at an old bivouac where some carcases of sheep and a few biscuits had been left lying about, but no other food was forthcoming. When the march was continued the road presented a depressing appearance. Of formed bodies of troops, except the Dorsets, there were few. Single guns, transport vehicles, and parties of stragglers blocked the road. Men of various units lay asleep by the roadside or sat about in groups trying to light fires. Little knots of stragglers crossed the open fields to cut off corners. Many stragglers had no rifles or equipment, and in some cases no cap badges, so that to identify their units was difficult. Confusion, weariness, and absence of orders and cohesion added to the gravity of the situation. At a road junction troops of a flank division converged on the main road making the confusion worse. Checks were frequent, and as the day advanced the sun grew very hot. The march discipline of the Dorsets was under the circumstances remarkably good, that of " D " Company particularly so. The officers, of whom Capt. Roe was as usual most noticeable, were untiring in their efforts to help and encourage the men. The experiences gained in Moore's Retreat to Corunna were again brought home. There the regiments which had fewest stragglers subsequently

31

gained the best record. Constant supervision by officers was essential then as now.

At 12.30 p.m. the Dorsets reached St. Quentin. The inhabitants appeared to be quite oblivious of the fact that a relentless enemy was at their gates. The streets were crowded with people following their normal occupations, while many idlers watched the troops with curiosity and apparent calm. Cafés were open and waiters stood at the doors napkin on arm.

Energetic efforts were being made by Staff Officers to sort out the many groups of stragglers from various divisions, and with success. The Dorsets halted at 1 p.m. in a field near the railway station, and it was understood that the march was over for the day. Shortly afterwards, however, orders were received for the retirement to be continued to the River Somme, and the march was resumed at 2 p.m. to Eaucourt, one mile W.S.W. of Ollezy, on the south bank, where the 15th Brigade went into bivouac. It is worthy of note that on this evening, 27th August, the 3rd and 5th Divisions were concentrated in the area about Ollezy with the River Somme between them and the pursuing enemy.

Since they commenced the retirement from Troisvilles on the afternoon of the 26th August until reaching this bivouac, the Dorsets had marched nearly 40 miles, on very little food and in intensely hot weather, on roads where frequent checks made marching unusually tiring. Yet few men fell out and straggling was not existent.

Before sunrise on the 28th August the retreat was continued, but it was unmolested by the enemy. There was a distinct improvement in the moral of the troops, though straggling was still prevalent in some battalions. The Commander-in-Chief (Sir John French) stood at the roadside to watch the troops pass. He exclaimed repeatedly: "You will have three days' rest." The march was continued via Guiscard, through Noyon—a fine old town—to Pontoise, on the south bank of the Oise, where the Dorsets bivouacked in an orchard. It had again been a tiring march, for the road was very hilly and the weather still extremely hot. Altogether a distance of 20 miles had been covered since leaving Eaucourt.

The following day, 29th August, no orders to move arrived, and it seemed that Sir John French's promise of three days' rest was to be fulfilled when the morning turned to afternoon. But shortly before 5 p.m. sudden orders came for a move of only 4 miles to Carlepont. On arrival in this village the main street was found hopelessly blocked by other troops and transport, and, as billeting was impossible, the men bivouacked along the village street and got little rest.

At 2.20 a.m. on the 30th August the retreat was resumed via Attichy on the Aisne to Croutoy. This was a very trying march, for the country, thickly wooded at first, opened out into open rolling downs without a vestige of shade. Croutoy was reached at 8 a.m., and the brigade halted on a ridge about 1 mile south of the village. There it remained until 12 noon, exposed to the midday sun, which seemed hotter than ever, when welcome orders were received that billets might be taken up in Croutoy which turned out to be a very comfortable and shady village.

At this time there was very little news. Nothing had been seen or heard of the Germans since the 26th August, and the reason for the continued retreat was not understood. The desire for one clear day and night's rest, with the possibility of a wash and shave, was uppermost in the minds of all ranks.

The 31st August was another tropical day. The march was resumed at 7.30 a.m., and lay in the direction of Compèigne Forest. This was a day of frequent long halts and checks, which made the march seem more than the 15 miles it actually was. The originally intended destination was Bèthisy, but the presence of hostile cavalry in its vicinity led to the line of march being diverted to Crèpy-en-Valois, which place was reached at 6 p.m., the troops going into bivouac. Thus 10½ hours had been occupied in covering 15 miles.

It had been intended to continue the retreat early on the 1st September, but before the move could begin, orders came for the brigade to proceed to Duvy. Arrived there, the Dorsets received orders to move to Rocquement in support of the 4th Division, but before the movement was completed it was cancelled, and the battalion returned to Duvy. The situation was very obscure, bodies of hostile cavalry being reported in the vicinity, but no fighting took place. The combat at Nery was responsible for these movements, though the

c

details of this action did not become generally known till later.

The Dorsets now marched across country to Ormoy Villers where they halted till 2 p.m., "B" and "D" Companies entrenching on the edge of the village. The retirement was then resumed to Nanteuil, where the battalion was ordered to find outposts in densely wooded country, "A," "B," and "C" Companies being so employed. The distance marched on this day was 12 miles in the same hot weather.

Starting at 4 a.m. on 2nd September the Dorsets marched to Montje as part of the rearguard of the 5th Division, but the march was unmolested. Montje was reached about noon after a 10-mile march, and billets were taken up. Montje was a pleasant and shady village on a hill-side.

The 3rd September was a particularly hot day, and saw a further rearward march of 15 miles across the Marne at Trilbardou, and thence by Esbly (where the 15th Brigade halted for an hour) to Mont Pichet. Here the Dorsets bivouacked and obtained a good night's rest, as no orders arrived for any march the following day.

The brigade remained in bivouac throughout the 4th September, though orders arrived in the afternoon for the retirement to be continued at 11.45 p.m., and after a tiring march of 16 miles, owing to checks in the darkness, the destination, Gagny, was reached. About 9 a.m. on the 5th good billets were found in the château, and all ranks obtained some welcome rest. Paris was now comparatively close, and rumour had it that the 5th Division was to go behind the forts to rest and refit. But as it happened Gagny formed the extreme limit of the Great Retreat as far as the Dorsets were concerned, for at 9 p.m. the following message arrived at Battalion Headquarters : "5th Division will resume the offensive to-morrow, marching about 5 a.m."

It is worthy of note that the "First Reinforcement" joined during the afternoon, consisting of 90 other ranks under command of Capt. Priestley.

VII

THE BATTLE OF THE MARNE

(See Maps C and X)

Northwards once more—Passage of the Petit Morin—Passage of the Marne—The Dorsets attack Hill 189—Capt. Roe's death—Comments on the fighting of 9th September, 1914.

At 5 a.m. on the 6th September the Dorsets began their march northwards once more, acting as advanced guard to the brigade. All ranks were in high spirits, and the marching was excellent. Distant gun-fire was audible from the north-east, but Mont Cerf was reached about 2 p.m. without incident—" C " and " D " Companies finding outposts. But at 6.45 p.m. the march was resumed, the Dorsets still as advanced guard, with orders to occupy some high ground about the line Le Charnois–Guerard. As it grew dark the advance became very slow, for the country was enclosed and difficult. A hostile cavalry patrol, encountered at La Celle, retired hastily after firing a few shots at the leading troops of " A " Company. The Dorsets halted just south of Villeneuve, covered by " A " Company. Heavy firing towards the right caused the Dorsets to stand to arms about 2 a.m., 7th September, but no action developed. At dawn two officers' patrols were sent forward, but found the front clear, and all remained quiet and no move took place till 12.45 p.m., when the Dorsets advanced through Tresmes towards Mouroux. About 3 p.m. just west of Mouroux two shells struck the road in front of the head of the battalion but caused no casualties, though the brigade was ordered to halt. The march was resumed at 4.45 p.m. via Coulommiers, which town showed many signs of recent German occupation, to Boissy Le Chatel, where the Dorsets bivouacked in an orchard.

Next morning, 8th September, one company of each battalion of the division was ordered to attend the execution of a deserter. This unpleasant duty fell to " B " Company. The march was resumed about 7.30 p.m. and went slowly, as the division was approaching the crossings of the Petit Morin, and the resistance of the

German rearguards was increasing. A halt of one hour took place at Doue, the 15th Brigade being in reserve. But the Dorsets were soon pushing on again through Mauroy, thence down a steep hill through St. Cyr and St. Ouen, across the Petit Morin, and thence up a steep hill. Rifle fire along the front was now general, and far away to the left a heavy fight was visible with many bursting shells and a few burning villages. Eventually the high ground to the front was cleared by other troops, and the Dorsets went into billets at Charnesseuil in some enormous barns.

Since leaving Gagny on the 6th the Dorsets had covered over 30 miles in the usual hot weather, though a heavy shower of rain had fallen during the evening of the 8th.

The 9th September was a day of great interest and importance, for it witnessed the passage of the Marne by the 5th Division, and culminated in very heavy fighting on the north bank during the afternoon. The 15th Brigade marched at 7.30 a.m.; it was a beautiful morning, and the early part of the march afforded a wonderful view for miles of the Marne Valley and the wooded heights on the northern bank. The bridge at Saacy was intact, and the brigade crossed without opposition and halted on the hill-side among the woods. Rifle and artillery fire could be heard to the front where the 14th Brigade, who were leading the 5th Division, had come in touch with hostile rearguards. After some delay the 15th Brigade, with the Dorsets leading, began at 11.30 a.m. to make their way forward through the woods, heading for Bezu, in order to turn the enemy's position on the Pisseloup Ridge. The column on emerging from the woods at Le Limon about noon was observed and shelled by the enemy from close range, but the Dorsets luckily escaped the shells which passed very close overhead. Lieut.-Col. Bols moved the men under cover of some orchards close at hand and proceeded to make a reconnaissance of Hill 189 (half a mile south-east of Montreuil), on which the enemy could be plainly seen entrenching. He reported to the brigade commander that he proposed to attack the hill, and the latter concurred, adding that he would send " B " Company, which had been detached earlier in the day with Brigade Headquarters, through the Bois des Essertis to turn the enemy's western flank. Lieut.-Col. Bols thereupon deployed " D " Company on the right and " C " Company on the left with Hill 189 as objective, reported that he was ready to attack and asked what artillery support he might expect. But artillery positions in this densely wooded region were hard to find, and, no support being forthcoming, the attack was launched without it at 2.30 p.m. Owing to the shape of the ground the battalion machine-guns could find no positions from which covering fire could be afforded, and the attack was therefore robbed of all support other than that which mutually supporting rifle fire could give.

The line of advance of " D " and " C " Companies lay over open stubble fields, exposed to heavy fire from machine-guns concealed in woods on either flank. The companies gained ground slowly by rushes, combined with rifle fire, but as a frontal attack unsupported by artillery fire it was doomed to failure from the outset, and by 3 p.m. " D " and " C " Companies were held up. " B " Company, meanwhile, made good progress through the Bois des Essertis, but they were unsupported, and soon became involved in heavy fighting. Their commander, Capt. Roe, was early wounded in the arm, but refused to leave his command, continuing to encourage his men, and to expose himself repeatedly. When he and his second-in-command, Capt. Priestley, were later mortally wounded, " B " Company's attack came finally to a standstill.

Capt. Roe died of his wounds some days later. The loss of this gallant and efficient officer was a severe blow. He had been adjutant of the battalion from 1908 to 1911, and had only recently graduated at the Staff College. Devoted to duty and to his battalion and unselfish to a degree, he will long be remembered. His gallant conduct was recognised by a posthumous mention in despatches.

Thus by 4 p.m. the Dorsets were lying in the open, engaged in a close-range fire fight with the enemy whose skilfully concealed machine-guns swept the open ground where the attacking lines lay and rendered movement practically impossible. Lieut. George, an able and efficient platoon commander of " D " Company, was mortally wounded as he raised himself to use his field-glasses ; Major Saunders, who throughout the attack behaved with great gallantry and exposed himself repeatedly to heavy fire, was also wounded ; luckily his wound was slight, and he was able to remain at duty.

" A " Company and Battalion Headquarters, who had moved off over the open close in rear of the leading companies when the attack started, were also pinned to the ground, and unable to manœuvre. About 4 p.m. the attacking troops were further harassed by a hostile field-howitzer battery which shelled the junction of the Dorsets with the 2nd Manchesters, causing the latter some casualties. Thus there ensued complete deadlock until nightfall.

As soon as it was dark the Dorsets were withdrawn into bivouac near Bezu, " A " and " C " Companies taking up covering positions. The casualties on this day were :

Wounded.—Capt. A. R. M. Roe (died of wounds), Capt. A. B. Priestley (died of wounds), Lieut. A. K. D. George (died of wounds), Major C. Saunders.

Other ranks.—Killed, 7 ; wounded, 31 ; missing, 4.

The 9th September was the critical day of the Battle of the Marne, and in this connection it is interesting to note that the pressure exerted by the 5th Division, with the 3rd Division on its right, throughout the day against the hastily organised force, Kraewel's Composite Brigade, thrown in to fill the gap in the German front, compelled the enemy to detach a division to strengthen the gap. This division was approaching the battlefield in the afternoon, when it was recalled to the northern flank to assist the German right. If it had been available for use against the French earlier in the day, it might have turned the scale. As it happened the pressure of the 2nd British Corps compelled its despatch elsewhere, as explained above, and it spent the day marching and counter-marching without firing a shot.

During the night 9th/10th September a warning order was received that the enemy was retiring northwards, and that the 15th Infantry Brigade was to advance on Montreuil at 4.30 a.m. on the 10th.

VIII

THE ADVANCE TO THE AISNE

Signs of German flight—Cooler weather—Nearing the Aisne—Passage by rafts—St. Marguerite and Missy—Billets at Jury—First relief of trenches—Missy—Withdrawal from the Aisne.

THE Dorsets as advanced guard to the brigade marched at 3.45 a.m. Montreuil was occupied by the 13th Infantry Brigade without opposition, and the Dorsets advanced through Dhuisy and Germigny. At the latter place two cavalry brigades, looking very smart and fresh, passed through to cover the advance. The wooded nature of the country necessitated a slow advance, and halts were frequent. A column of German transport, seen moving on a parallel road, was shelled by our guns and dispersed in confusion. After a halt at Germigny the column pushed on to Gandelu, and here were visible numerous signs of a hurried German retreat in the shape of hastily vacated bivouacs, a derelict motor-car, dead men and horses, and quantities of discarded equipment. On approaching Chezy, a splendid natural defensive position for the enemy if he had had time to organise it—he had, in fact, dug trenches—the column halted near a long convoy of broken wagons, previously overtaken by our cavalry. By brigade permission the troops were allowed to help themselves to the contents. On reaching Chezy the Dorsets had to halt as the road was blocked by troops of the 3rd Division, whose line of march passed through it. The weather had now turned wet, heavy showers falling at intervals. After some delay the Dorsets moved on towards a thick wood and a large farm named St. Quentin. More delay was caused, but this time by our own heavy guns which persisted in shelling the wood for over an hour. Finally, about sunset, the Dorsets bivouacked at the farm. At 7.30 p.m. the second reinforcement, strength 187, with Lieut. Parkinson and 2/Lieut. Clutterbuck, joined. A distance of 16 miles was covered during the day in much colder weather, punctuated during the afternoon by very heavy thunder showers.

The 11th September calls for little comment, for it

entailed a march of 11 miles via Marizy St. Genevieve–
Marizy St. Mard–Billy–Chouy without opposition. The
weather had become very wet, but the cooler air was
agreeable after the long spell of intense heat. The
Dorsets found very comfortable billets at St. Remy.

The 12th September was a long tiring day of many
halts. The British Army was now approaching the south
bank of the Aisne, and fighting was in progress at many
points along the front, though the 15th Infantry Brigade
was not engaged. A long halt took place on an open
wind-swept plateau just south of the Ferme de l'Epitaphe.
The troops sat huddled together in the pouring rain until
6 p.m. when the Dorsets were ordered to march back to
Namteuil, through which village they had passed in the
morning, and billet there. After a serious block in the
village while the rain poured down, driven in sheets by a
gale that had sprung up, quarters were at last found for
all, though there was much overcrowding.

After an uncomfortable night the Dorsets marched
again at 4 a.m. on the 13th September, and by 5 a.m.
were in reserve at Mont de Soissons Farm (1½ miles
south of Serches) to the 13th Infantry Brigade, then
engaged in attacking the bridge over the Aisne at Missy.

The weather had improved, but the wind was still high
and very cold after the recent heat wave. By 8 a.m. the
15th Infantry Brigade had reached the high ground
close to Serches, overlooking the Aisne valley. Here the
brigade remained for hours, though the battalions had
to be moved a short distance at 2.45 p.m. to avoid hostile
shells. The weather improved further and the sun came
out, but it remained chilly. Just when it was expected
that the troops would go into bivouac, orders arrived
that the brigade was to cross the Aisne during the night.
The Dorsets marched at 8 p.m. to the Moulin des Roches
(see Map D) and commenced the passage at midnight.
Two rafts had been constructed by the Royal Engineers,
each carrying about 50 men, so that the passing of the
whole brigade across the river was a slow operation,
taking in all over four hours.

In the light of after events, it seems extraordinary
that the passage of a whole brigade by means of two rafts,
constructed and used the previous day, and the point of
passage therefore known to the enemy, should have been
unmolested. The Germans had masses of artillery on

the wooded heights about Chivres and Vregny (see Map D), but at that time they did no night firing. Such an operation as the passage of a big river in face of an enemy, alert and in prepared positions on the far bank, would have been a well-nigh impossible operation from 1915 onwards. As it was, the brigade formed up on the north bank in some marshy fields without incident and tried to sleep.

On 14th September, at 4 a.m., the brigade, with the Dorsets leading, advanced via the eastern end of Bucy le Long towards St. Marguerite. Although it was growing light, the masses of troops, moving in artillery formation, appeared to escape notice, and it was not till the latter village had been reached that hostile shelling commenced, but then the shelter of the houses prevented casualties from the shrapnel shells which the Germans used. At 7 a.m. Lieut.-Col. Bols moved the Dorsets into a deep sunken lane with wooded slopes running north-west from the northern edge of St. Marguerite, while the remainder of the brigade remained in the village which was now being heavily shelled. In front were the 14th Infantry Brigade on the right, and the 12th Infantry Brigade (4th Division) on the left, and when, at 12 noon, Brig.-Gen. Count Gleichen decided to move to Missy, in accordance with his original orders, the Dorsets remained to fill the gap between these two brigades. All the afternoon St. Marguerite was heavily shelled, and a number of artillery horses were killed in the village street. The sunken lane in which the Dorsets were was also shelled and a number of casualties were suffered.

The attack by the 15th Infantry Brigade (less the Dorsets) on the Chivres spur failed, for it was unsupported by artillery and had to be made through thickly wooded country. By dusk the shelling died away, and Lieut.-Col. Bols ordered the Dorsets into billets at St. Marguerite at 7 p.m. Casualties amounted to twenty wounded, all by shell-fire. The weather had been cold and showery all day.

At 4 a.m., 15th September, the Dorsets moved out of billets; Headquarters, " A," and " C " Companies to the sunken lane, and " B " and " D " Companies to the slope in rear of it, where they entrenched themselves. Meanwhile the attack of the Chivres spur by the 15th Infantry Brigade was resumed.

All the morning the Dorsets were shelled, and repeated casualties were caused.

At 1 p.m. orders arrived for the Dorsets to move to Missy to rejoin the 15th Infantry Brigade. At 2 p.m. the move commenced. " A " Company was directed to occupy a small hill about 600 yards east of the 14th Infantry Brigade Headquarters (known as Rolt's Farm) with " C " Company in support. In carrying out this movement " A " Company came under machine-gun fire and suffered casualties. Meanwhile " B " and " D " Companies moved across the enemy's front, passing across the open fields parallel to the St. Marguerite–Missy Road, and occupied a line from La Bezaie Farm to the mill on the St. Marguerite–Missy Road. This movement, incredible as it may seem, was completed without hostile interruption, though in full view. At 5 p.m. " B " and " D " Companies commenced to dig in with their small entrenching tools in the vicinity of Bezaie Farm.

At 9 p.m. orders arrived that the 15th Infantry Brigade was to withdraw south of the Aisne and go into billets. The adjutant was despatched to order the companies to assemble at La Bezaie Farm, and the battalion was concentrated at that place by 10 p.m. Marching in column of route it moved to the river and crossed by a newly constructed pontoon bridge. Once more there was no hostile shelling, but the enemy used the searchlight persistently, and heavy rifle fire could be heard at Missy. The Dorsets had one man killed and twenty-one wounded on this day. By 1 a.m., 16th September, the battalion had reached its billets at Jury.

The days that followed were uneventful. The Dorsets were kept busy entrenching along the Sermoise–Soissons Road and in preparing a position on the plateau overlooking the Aisne north-east of Jury. The weather remained chilly and unsettled. At 7.30 p.m. on the 20th September sudden orders for the Dorsets to proceed at once to Sermoise were issued and almost immediately cancelled. However, at 7.30 p.m. on 21st September orders to proceed at once to Rapreux Farm were not cancelled, and the Dorsets (less " C " and " D " Companies, already in trenches on the river bank about Sermoise) marched at 8.10 p.m. Orders to bivouac at Rapreux Farm, and to be prepared to move to Missy early on 22nd September, arrived at 10.30 p.m., but an hour later these were cancelled, and the Dorsets were ordered to return to Jury. But on 22nd September orders arrived that the Dorsets were to relieve the East Surreys at Missy after dark. Once again the orders were cancelled. But they were renewed at 10 a.m. on 23rd September, and at 6 p.m. the Dorsets set out to carry out the first of many reliefs they were destined to take part in France and Belgium in the years to follow.

This event marks the beginning of trench warfare, though no one could have foretold it at the time. With great caution and in complete silence the Dorsets, in column of route, and guided by Major Saunders, crossed the Aisne by the pontoon bridge and moved to Missy. " A " and " B " Companies took over the advanced trenches, such as they were, " C " and " D " Companies occupying houses in Missy. Lieut.-Col. Bols took command of two sections of the front, consisting of Missy village, the 2nd Duke of Wellingtons being on the right and the Dorsets on the left.

Life at Missy was not particularly eventful, even though it was somewhat novel. But regarded in the light of the many lessons learnt by the British Army in the years of war to follow, it seems strange that two battalions, unprotected by wire entanglements, poorly entrenched, and unprovided with dug-outs, which at that date had not been heard of, should have been crowded together in a village within a few hundred yards of the enemy, with an unfordable river crossed by only one bridge in rear of them, and with no supporting troops to be called upon if required. Ignorance is bliss, no doubt, and there were few who realised the gravity of the position, but Lieut.-Col. Bols was fully alive to the situation. He caused deep trenches to be dug in the gardens of the cottages used as billets, until cover was provided for all. He set a definite programme of work in motion, with a result that an excellent deep trench was constructed, giving covered lateral communication on the battalion front. He also recommended to Brigade Headquarters that further bridges should be constructed to facilitate the passage of reinforcements should the latter be necessary at any time. Major Saunders, always to the fore in matters of field engineering, busied himself with many details of defence construction and caused a formidable stone barricade to be erected blocking the village street. Another peculiar feature of this period was the nightly visit of many transport vehicles with supplies, which arrived after dark at Missy village under Major and Quartermaster Kearney. This transport crossed the Aisne by Venizel Bridge and marched thence via St. Marguerite, passing within a few hundred yards of the hostile front line, and at certain points in front of the British front line.

But a few events did occur to enliven the monotony of the Dorsets' tour of duty at Missy. The first took the form of a message received on the afternoon of the 25th September, which stated that, in view of the possibility of a German attack during the coming forty-eight hours, every possible precaution was to be taken. No attack occurred however.

But before dawn on the 27th September news arrived that the Duke of Wellingtons at Gobinn Wood reported the enemy to be crossing Condé Bridge in large numbers. This was supplemented at 4 a.m. by an order from Brigade Headquarters repeating the report and ordering the Dorsets to stand to arms. It should be noted that Condé Bridge was still in German hands. The report turned out to be false. But this day, a Sunday, was not to pass without incident, for at 10.45 a.m. the enemy commenced a concentrated bombardment of Missy village with shells of all calibres, and this continued until dusk. However, the troops in the village took shelter in their deep trenches and escaped without a single casualty. Although Missy was subjected to intermittent shelling daily following the Sunday bombardment, no other events of interest occurred until news arrived on 1st October that the Dorsets were to be relieved by the 1st Essex (4th Division) and go into billets at Jury once more. The relief was accomplished without incident.

During the period 23rd September to 1st October not a single casualty had been suffered by the Dorsets. The deep trenches had fulfilled their purpose beyond expectation. Nor must the excellent discipline displayed by all ranks in avoiding all unnecessary movement by day at exposed points—always a difficult order to enforce—be lost sight of.

IX

THE MOVE TO FLANDERS

(SEE MAPS X, E, F AND G)

Secrecy—Northwards by train—A 'bus journey—Bethune—The Battle
of La Bassée begins—The Dorsets' advance—Major Roper killed
—Situation at nightfall 12th October, 1914—The fighting on
13th October, 1914, at Pont Fixe—A desperate situation—Withdrawal—Lieut.-Col. Bols' escape—A new line established—Pont
Fixe held—Relief—In reserve—The fighting at Violaines on
22nd October, 1914—Arrival of the Indians—Farewell to Givenchy
—Festubert.

To understand the reasons for the long marches that
took place in the first weeks of October, 1914, it is
necessary to summarise shortly the existing situation on
the left of the Allied line at that period. The German
retreat had come to a halt on a strong natural and previously prepared position, but north of Arras the flanks
of the contending armies were merely covered by cavalry.
Both opposing Higher Commands perceived the opportunity which this situation offered of out-flanking the
other. Thus both sides began to hurry troops to their
northern flank, and there followed what has been
described as the " Race to the Sea." Sir John French
obtained permission to move the British Expeditionary
Force to the Allied left flank as soon as it could be
relieved by French troops, in order to shorten his lines
of communication with the coast.

So in the first days of October the movement commenced. The utmost secrecy was maintained. No hint
of the actual destination was given. The wildest rumours
were in circulation ; Antwerp and even England were
suggested as the ultimate goal. The Dorsets marched
at 7 p.m. on the 2nd October a distance of nine miles to
Launoy and went into billets at midnight, though delayed
by fog, and after spending the day resting, moved on
again at 6 p.m. and reached their billets at Corcy
about midnight after covering 11 miles. Marching at
7 p.m. on the 4th October a long delay occurred, while
columns of French troops crossed the Dorsets' line of
march. Billets at Fresnoy la Riviere were reached
about 5 a.m. on the 5th October, after a march of 17

miles.   On this day Lieut. Pitt took over the duties of adjutant from Capt. Ransome whose tenure of the appointment had expired.   No further move took place till 2.45 p.m. on the 6th October.   A march of 10 miles followed to Verberie (not far from Crèpy en Valois, passed by the Dorsets during the Retreat from Mons).

This marked the close of the series of night marches conducted with great secrecy, the daytime being spent with all troops confined to their billets to avoid observations from the air.   Orders to entrain at Compiegne arrived, and the Dorsets left Verberie at 3 a.m. on the 7th October.   Compiegne was reached at 7 a.m., and the train conveying the Dorsets left at 11 a.m.   Amiens and Abbeville were reached in turn, but, as there was congestion at the latter place, the train was sent back to Pont Rèmy, where, after delay, the Dorsets detrained under great difficulties, no facilities existing for unloading vehicles.   By 2 a.m., 8th October, the detrainment was completed, and the Dorsets marched via Abbeville to Neuilly.   By 6 p.m. the same day the Dorsets were on the march once more and reached their billets at Genne Ivergny about 11 p.m.

On the afternoon of the 9th October it was made known that the infantry of the 5th Division were to be sent north in French 'buses, the transport to move independently.   Consequently the Dorsets moved at 5 p.m. to Haravesnes where the 'buses were to assemble, and went into billets, moving out at 3 a.m. on the 10th October to the embussing point.   But experience in moving large bodies of troops by this means was lacking in 1914, and no motor vehicles arrived till 2.30 p.m. The convoy moved via St. Pol to Dièval near La Thieuloye, to which village the Dorsets marched and went into billets.   On the 9th October Capt. Ransome had, as a temporary measure, taken over command of the machine-gun section, vice Lieut. Woodhouse, sick.

As the Dorsets were now close to their new battle front, and indeed heavy gun-fire had been heard for some days past, it may be well to say here how the battalion fared at the moment as regards numbers and moral. Well supplied with reinforcements and fortunate perhaps in the past in not suffering very heavy casualties, though several valuable officers had been lost, the battalion was at full strength, and its fighting spirit was excellent.   No one could dream that in the short space of five days it would be reduced, in what was perhaps its severest ordeal in the whole war, to a mere skeleton, and that months must necessarily elapse before it recovered its efficiency as a fighting machine.

In a great war in which the whole manhood of nations is called into service, the ranks will be filled again and again, but no new blood, whatever its enthusiasm, bravery, and physical advantages, can compensate for the loss of that spirit which is engendered by the comradeship of all ranks in times of peace. By the end of October, 1914, the old Army which had borne the burden and heat of those terrible days of the first August of the war had passed away.

About 8 a.m. on the 11th October the Dorsets set out for their next destination—Bethune. Their route lay through Bruay, a big mining town, and the character of the country began to change. Reminders of the Mons district were visible on every hand—tall chimneys, rows of miners' dwellings, slag heaps in profusion. But Bethune was a pleasant enough town, providing splendid billets into which Headquarters and " A " and " D " Companies settled themselves by 7 p.m., with " B " and " C " Companies providing outposts along the Aire–Bethune Canal.

The 12th October saw a dense white fog enveloping the low-lying country eastwards of Bethune, the fields of which were intersected with dykes fringed with willows. Numerous large farms were dotted about and the pastures were well stocked with cattle. Another feature of the countryside was the narrow *pavé* roads.

The orders for the Dorsets on this day, which was to see the opening of the great battle in Flanders culminating in the First Battle of Ypres, were to march to the line Festubert–Rue de l'Epinette (see Map E). These orders were in pursuance of the plan of the IInd Corps commander to pin down the enemy with the 5th Division, while the 3rd Division on its left wheeled westwards against La Bassee. The 15th Infantry Brigade, therefore, marched at 8.30 a.m. covered by the Cheshires as advanced guard. Moving by Gorre in the dense fog, the Dorsets halted south of the Rue de Bethune, known afterwards from 1915 onwards as the " Tuning Fork," from the shape of two parallel roads converging at

Gorre. A few shells were bursting at intervals along the
Festubert–Rue de l'Epinette Road, but there were no
signs of hostile infantry. As the flank of the 15th Brigade
had been ordered to rest on the La Bassee Canal, the
Dorsets were diverted along the canal tow-path to Pont
Fixe, the bridge over the canal at Cuinchy railway
station. The Pont Fixe–Le Plantin Road was held by a
battalion of French Territorials, and " A " and " D "
Companies proceeded to relieve these troops, " A "
Company occupying a brewery just south of the canal,
and " D " Company the houses on the north side.
Observers reported Germans in the brickfields east of
Cuinchy, and a machine-gun was placed in position on
the first floor of a big unfinished factory on the north bank
of the canal. This gun engaged with success parties of
Germans debouching from the brickfields, and later
enfiladed and caused to retire a line of Germans advancing
towards Cuinchy against the French troops south of the
canal. No sign of Germans could be seen on the north
side of the canal, though a good view of the country as
far as La Bassee was obtainable from the factory. The
situation south of the canal was uncertain. French
troops could be seen advancing towards Cuinchy, which
by early afternoon must have been in occupation by
hostile advanced troops.

Nevertheless, at 3.30 p.m. the Dorsets were ordered to
advance on La Bassee, in conjunction with the Bedfords
at Givenchy and the Cheshires at La Quinque Rue.
Accordingly " A " Company moved along the southern
tow-path of the canal under cover of the high railway
embankment, and, supported by overhead machine-gun
fire, made good progress, encountering and causing
casualties to a large party of Germans whom they sur-
prised with their fire. In leading this advance Lieut.
Lilly was wounded. Meanwhile " D " Company moved
forward from Pont Fixe towards a large farm about 200
yards east of the factory, but when crossing the inter-
vening root field they encountered a cross rifle fire from
the direction of Cuinchy and suffered some loss. As their
advance from the farm enclosures was temporarily held
up, Major Roper went forward to reconnoitre. He was
almost immediately hit in the head and died shortly
afterwards.

Major Roper's death was not only a great loss to his

battalion, but in a still greater degree to the whole Army. He had had many years' experience in important Staff appointments and was a very accomplished officer. Had he lived, he would without doubt have risen to a high position in his profession.

By nightfall the advance of the Dorsets had made good progress, and a general line had been established from the canal, thence east of the farm above referred to, to another big farm and orchard standing on a small rise on the southern edge of Givenchy. This line was occupied by " B " Company on the right and " C " Company on the left, and the men began to dig in. " A " and " D " Companies were withdrawn to Pont Fixe ; " A " Company to the brewery on the south bank of the canal. The Bedfords had occupied Givenchy and were in touch with " C " Company.

During the day the Dorsets lost 11 killed and 30 wounded in addition to Major Roper and Lieut. Lilly.

Here it is well to pause and consider for a moment the general situation on this part of the front. Except for cavalry, which was certainly not in evidence on the 12th October, it is now known that the Germans had no infantry close to the British front on the north bank of the La Bassee Canal. Their real right flank therefore rested at Cuinchy on the night 12th/13th October. But Lille had fallen some days previously, and by the 12th German troops were being hurried forward to the La Bassee area to meet the threatened enveloping movement caused by the deployment on the 12th October of the 5th Division on the line Pont Fixe–Richbourg l'Avoué. So by midday on the 13th October it should be noted that the situation north of the La Bassee Canal showed a gradual increase in the hostile resistance, culminating in a German advance.

But for a considerable time on the 13th October the opposing hostile troops consisted of Jäger with machine-guns, and dismounted cavalry, supported by an increasing number of guns.

Orders from Brigade Headquarters arrived during the night for the advance to be resumed at 5.30 a.m. " B " Company on the right and " C " Company on the left were to lead, with " D " Company in close support and " A " Company in reserve.

Accordingly at 5.30 a.m. the advance commenced, and

D

the platoons of Lieut. Turner, " B " Company, and Lieut. Fraser, " C " Company, reached the line of a track bordered by willows. But as the light grew stronger, and the mist began to disperse, hostile resistance began to manifest itself. A cross fire was directed against our advanced line from the south, and " B " Company in particular began to suffer. Hostile guns also opened fire from the direction of Rue d'Ouvert. One machine-gun of the Dorsets had been moved forward at dawn to the upper room of a small house at the lock, where it could sweep the southern canal bank, and the exits from the brickfields, but owing to the flat nature of the country north of the canal, overhead fire in support of " B " and " C " Companies was impossible. But a hostile Machine-gun brought to the canal bank to enfilade " B " Company was engaged at a range of five hundred yards and never fired again. Other targets were engaged with success.

Lieut.-Col. Bols was anxious about his flanks, for no touch could be gained on the right with the 13th Infantry Brigade, expected to be at Cuinchy, and a gap appeared to exist between the Dorsets and the Bedfords at Givenchy. He therefore felt that he could not push on until the troops on his flanks came up into line. The Dorsets remained throughout the morning exposed to a galling cross fire from the south. Lieuts. Turner and Fraser became casualties early. Later Capt. Kitchin, commanding " B " Company, was wounded and 2/Lieut. Smith killed. These two officers had joined the battalion on the Aisne. Sergt. Boater (No. 5 platoon) very pluckily climbed a tree in order to engage hostile riflemen lining the canal bank, but in his exposed position he was very soon killed. The enemy located the Dorsets' machine-gun firing from the cottage window, and one man was hit at once, so work on the construction of a loop-hole in the southern wall was commenced, as all attempts to use the window were frustrated by unseen riflemen.

As " B " Company's position was gradually becoming untenable, they were ordered to withdraw along the canal to Pont Fixe. Many men were killed and wounded in this withdrawal, which began about noon, from close-range fire from the southern canal bank.

The Germans had now brought up a field howitzer battery which concentrated upon " D " Company, lying in the open in rear of the front companies, and upon a forward section of 18-pounders which was under cover of the spoil bank close to Battalion Headquarters. Lieut. Parkinson (" D " Company) was killed instantaneously, and a number of others were hit. The situation appeared to be critical, since the enemy was undoubtedly gaining ground about Cuinchy, and that flank was now open owing to the withdrawal of " B " Company from its untenable position. Heavy rifle fire was also coming from the direction of Givenchy. As it was known that the line Pont Fixe–Le Plantin was unoccupied except by stragglers, Capt. Beveridge and Capt. Ransome, after consultation, decided to withdraw " A " Company, then under cover in the sunken road running from the canal lock to Givenchy, to positions at Pont Fixe held on the 12th October, so as to form a line on which troops could rally, if a general withdrawal became necessary. The machine-gun was to follow when " A " Company was in position. This difficult movement was successfully carried out under heavy cross fire, and a line taken up at Pont Fixe where a position was being organised by Major Saunders.

Meanwhile, events about Givenchy, which had been heavily shelled since morning, culminated in an attack upon the left rear of " C " Company whose left trench was overrun. Lieut.-Col. Bols and the Adjutant (Lieut. Pitt) engaged the advancing enemy with rifles taken from casualties, but the odds were too great, and Lieut.-Col. Bols was severely wounded and taken prisoner and Lieut. Pitt and Capt. Davidson killed.

Lieut.-Col. Bols had an extraordinary experience. After being attended to by a German stretcher bearer, he was left unattended while an ambulance was sent for, and was able to crawl and struggle back to our lines at Pont Fixe in the darkness.

The two forward 18-pounders fell into the enemy's hands. These guns were worked to the last by their detachments who all became casualties, assisted by Capt. Rathborne and several men of the Dorsets, all of whom displayed great gallantry. Capt. Rathborne was severely wounded, but managed to crawl back to Pont Fixe.

By 4 p.m. a line had been firmly established along the road from the canal bridge towards Le Plantin where touch was gained with the Bedfords. " A " Company occupied the factory and houses near the bridge, while a machine-gun was brought into action in a farm about 300 yards along the road towards Le Plantin, whence it opened fire on Givenchy village. Efforts to use the top floor of the factory—this gun's position throughout the afternoon of the 12th October—had been frustrated at once by hostile artillery which had obtained two direct hits on the building as soon as the gun had opened fire on Cuinchy.

Major Saunders had now assumed command and had established his headquarters in an *estaminet* at Pont Fixe. Capt. Ransome resumed the duties of adjutant in place of Lieut. Pitt, handing over command of the machine-gun section to Sergt. Gambling. Two companies of the Devons were on their way to support the Dorsets, and by nightfall the situation was well in hand and the canal bridge secured.

In his despatch of the 20th November, 1914, Sir John French refers to the fighting of the 13th October as follows :

" On and after the 13th October the object of the G.O.C. Second Corps was to wheel to his right pivoting on Givenchy to get astride the La Bassée–Lille Road in the neighbourhood of Fournes, so as to threaten the right flank and rear of the enemy's position on the high ground south of La Bassée.

This position of La Bassée has throughout the battle defied all attempts at capture, either by the French or the British.

On this day Sir Horace Smith-Dorrien could make but little progress. He particularly mentions the fine fighting of the Dorsets. They suffered no less than 400 casualties, 130 of them being killed, but maintained all day their hold on Pont Fixe."

The casualties on this day were terribly heavy. Among the officers Capt. Davidson, Lieut. and Adjutant Pitt, Lieuts. Parkinson, Turner, and Smith were killed. Besides Lieut.-Col. Bols, Capt. Kitchin, Capt. Rathborne, and Lieut. Fraser were wounded. The latter fell into the hands of the Germans, and was left for days in a neglected state in La Bassee. Capt. Kelsall, Lieuts. Grant-Dalton and Clutterbuck, all of " C " Company, whose position was overrun from the rear as already described, were also made prisoners. Among other ranks

the casualty returns showed 51 killed, 152 wounded, and
210 missing. Of the missing many killed or wounded
were left on the battlefield. Two able and experienced
warrant officers, C.S.M.'s Gould and Parker, were among
the killed.

The night passed quietly, and daylight on the 14th
October found "A" Company holding the factory at
Pont Fixe, with their left prolonged by two companies of
the 1st Devons. The remnants of "B," "C," and "D"
Companies had been formed into a composite company
under Capt. Beveridge who had 2/Lieuts. Wiltshire, King,
and Butcher to assist him. This company was placed
under cover of a ditch with its right on the canal bank,
about half a mile west of Pont Fixe, to act as a support if
required. "A" Company in the factory were heavily
shelled all day. The importance of the canal bridge was
emphasised by a message received from the 15th Brigade
which read: "Pont Fixe must not be given up. I know
I can rely on you to stick to it with the help of the
Devons."

Meanwhile, south of the canal, an attack on Vermelles
by the French was in preparation and was timed to
commence at 2 p.m. In this attack the Dorsets and the
Devons were ordered to co-operate, but Major Saunders,
bearing in mind the lesson learnt on the previous day,
instructed "A" Company not to advance from its
position at Pont Fixe until the attack on the south side
of the canal at Cuinchy commenced. This reservation
was very necessary, as a premature advance would have
again exposed the right flank to enfilade fire from the
enemy occupying Cuinchy. The attack by the French
did not develop, but the enemy took the offensive on the
front of the 13th Brigade, west of Cuinchy; so all idea of
a renewed forward movement was abandoned for the
day. After dark, at about 8.30 p.m., the enemy made a
local attack upon "A" Company holding the Pont Fixe
factory, but was repulsed.

On this day Major Saunders caused a barge to be towed
down the canal and fixed in position so that it could be
used as a bridge at a point sheltered from hostile view,
for the bridge at Pont Fixe was now under direct machine-
gun fire. There was considerable rifle fire throughout
the hours of darkness, but no further attack after that
mentioned as taking place at 8.30 p.m.

The 15th October saw no change on the Dorsets' front. " A " Company's positions were again violently shelled, but there was no hostile attack. Our guns bombarded Givenchy heavily, and the village was being rapidly reduced to ruins. Meanwhile the French were attacking Vermelles south of the canal, and orders had been received for an advance north of the canal to begin as soon as their attack succeeded. But they made no progress, and it was therefore impossible to advance north of the canal. Orders had been received that the Devons were to relieve the Dorsets after dark, and by 7.30 p.m. they had done so. " A " Company, who had done splendid work in the defence of the factory under trying conditions, were withdrawn along the northern canal bank, where they joined the remnants of " B," " C," and " D " Companies, and the march was continued via Gorre to Loisne (see Map G) where billets were taken up. It was hoped to gain some much-needed rest and to reorganise generally, but during the night orders arrived from the 13th Brigade, to which the Dorsets were now attached, for the battalion to rendezvous just east of the Rue de Bethune hamlet by 6 a.m., 16th October, there to be in Divisional Reserve. The Dorsets remained in the open in this position till dusk, when billets were taken up in Festubert which up to then had hardly been shelled.

By 7 a.m., 17th October, the Dorsets were back again at their rendezvous of the previous day, and returned to Festubert in the evening.

After returning to the old rendezvous once more at 6 a.m. on the 18th October, the Dorsets were ordered to march at 10 a.m. to Chapelle St. Roch. During the time they had been in Divisional Reserve at Festubert, the advance of the 3rd Division further north had caused the Germans to withdraw from Givenchy which had become a pronounced salient to their line. By the evening of the 17th October the 15th Brigade had advanced to the line Canteleux–Violaines. This advance had enabled Major Saunders to obtain permission to send a burial party under Lieut. Woodhouse, who had returned to duty on the 15th, to the Dorsets' battlefield of 13th October. This party buried about 100 dead.

The Dorsets concentrated at Chapelle St. Roch after marching via La Quinque Rue and Rue d'Ouvert. When approaching the latter place the column was noticed by hostile observers, for the country was quite flat and devoid of cover, and eight heavy shells fell by the roadside without, however, doing any damage. At 6 p.m. billets were taken up in Rue d'Ouvert.

The Dorsets remained in this position, still in Divisional Reserve, until the afternoon of the 20th October. Beyond considerable hostile shelling of Rue d'Ouvert each evening nothing of interest occurred. At 2 p.m., 20th October, the Dorsets were ordered to a position under cover of a slight rise a few hundred yards east of Rue d'Ouvert. Hostile attacks were now threatening upon the Cheshires, who held a somewhat exposed position at Violaines, and the Dorsets were now in close support of them. At 7 p.m. the Composite company commenced to entrench on the rise above mentioned, but were withdrawn at 11 p.m., together with " A " Company, to farms at Rue du Marais. At 5.30 a.m. on the 21st October heavy rifle fire was heard from Violaines, and " A " Company was despatched to a position along the Chapelle St. Roch–Rue du Marais Road in rear of the Bedfords, who held the front on the Cheshires' right. This was a day of many rumours ; but it was clear by dusk that the Germans had been strongly reinforced and had pressed back the 14th Brigade from Lorgies, leaving the Cheshires' left flank still more exposed. Digging tasks under R.E. supervision were allotted to both " A " and the Composite company that night.

The 22nd October was an anxious day. At 5.30 a.m. loud cheering from the direction of Violaines (see Map F) was clearly heard at the Dorsets' headquarters at Rue du Marais. This was followed by heavy rifle fire and the retirement of several transport vehicles through Rue du Marais. It appeared that the enemy had made a surprise attack on the Cheshires' advanced posts and had driven them in, overrunning other troops who at this time were busily engaged in digging. The hostile advance rapidly rendered untenable the unfinished trench at which the Composite company were working, as it was badly enfiladed from the north side of Violaines. Capt. Beveridge was wounded and taken prisoner, and Lieut. King wounded. Lieut. Woodhouse, who had been sent by Major Saunders with one machine-gun to Violaines before dawn, was reconnoitring when the Germans attacked and was involved at once in the confusion. He made gallant efforts to rally stragglers and to direct fire against the assailants, but was soon surrounded by Germans who had entered the village from the north, unseen in the dim light, and was taken prisoner. The machine-gun was lost, though it was hurriedly concealed under some straw.

To meet the situation the Battalion Reserve, consisting of one platoon under C.S.M. Holloway, was placed to block the eastern end of Rue du Marais, and the remaining machine-gun came into action just south of the village. Under cover of these the men of various units were collected and reformed, for companies had become very scattered in the sudden confusion caused by the surprise attack. It should be borne in mind that the majority of the troops in this sector had been in action incessantly for ten days with no rest, and had moreover been actually digging, disposed at wide intervals, when overrun in the dull morning light. Major Saunders decided that, as reinforcements in the shape of two battalions were approaching Rue du Marais, presumably to counter-attack, it would be better to withdraw the men he had collected to La Quinque Rue, where there would be better facilities for reorganisation than in a village under direct machine-gun fire. By 7 a.m. "A" Company, less 2/Lieut. Shannon's platoon, which did not rejoin till after dark, had been reorganised, together with remnants of the Composite company and elements of the Bedfords and the Cheshires. Meanwhile, our guns shelled Violaines very heavily, but our infantry counter-attacks could not get beyond Rue du Marais. Still, these troops had the effect of checking the Germans for the rest of the day.

At 8 p.m. the Dorsets were withdrawn to billets at Festubert. This unsatisfactory day cost the battalion the following casualties : Capt. Beveridge, wounded and missing ; Lieut. Woodhouse, missing ; Lieuts. King and Butcher, wounded. *Other ranks.*—7 killed, 22 wounded, 101 missing.

Until the 27th October nothing of any special importance occurred as far as the Dorsets were concerned. On the 23rd they were moved to billets at Rue de Bethune (see Map G), assembling at their rendezvous of the 16th and 17th at 6.30 p.m. in readiness for eventualities and remaining in the open all night. This procedure was repeated on the 24th October. At this time there were frequent complaints that our men had been fired on behind the lines ; also many inhabitants of Festubert were suspected of being enemy agents. Many of the incidents reported were without foundation, but it is perfectly reasonable to assume that spies were actually at work during this period, as the inhabitants had been allowed by the French authorities to remain in their houses close behind the firing line.

At 4 p.m. on the 25th October the battalion was alarmed and moved to its position of readiness, but the expected attack did not materialise. It should be noted that after the fighting on the 22nd the front of the 5th Division was withdrawn to a line running east of Givenchy through La Quinque Rue to Richbourg l'Avoue, and during the days that followed hostile attacks were frequently made and were always expected against this new front. The 25th October found the Dorsets located at Gorre, as Rue de Bethune was becoming very " unhealthy " owing to heavy hostile shelling. The village of Festubert in particular was heavily shelled daily. This day was spent in digging a reserve line in the vicinity of Rue de Bethune.

About this date commissions in the Dorsetshire Regiment were granted to C.S.M. Holloway (" C " Company), Sergt. S. W. Miller (" A " Company), and Sergt. Sigrist (" B " Company).

The Dorsets moved on the 27th at 6 a.m. to Le Touret, and there in the afternoon they received a welcome reinforcement of 5 officers and 310 other ranks. But no time was available to allot these new arrivals to companies, as a sudden order arrived at 6.15 p.m. for a move to Richbourg l'Avoue. This draft remained at Le Touret under Capt. Fraser.

It transpired that Neuve Chapelle had that day been lost, and that it was intended to retake it by a night counter-attack.

Besides the Dorsets, the Cheshires and D.C.L.I. (both very weak in numbers), and two companies of the Bedfords assembled at Richbourg l'Avoue. It was proposed that this force should carry out the counter-attack under the command of Brig.-Gen. Maude, then commanding the 14th Brigade. While the troops waited along the road in Richbourg l'Avoue, a conference was held, and it was finally decided that owing to the darkness and the fact that no reconnaissance of the approaches to Neuve Chapelle was possible, the night counter-attack would not be proceeded with.

The troops remained all night by the roadside waiting until this decision was arrived at, and at 6 a.m. on the 28th the Dorsets moved together with the other battalions to a position close to the La Bassee–Estaires Road, east of Richbourg St. Vaast, where they remained throughout the day under cover of damp ditches, while an attack was launched by troops attached to the 7th Brigade, notably a dismounted cavalry regiment, and a Sikh battalion. These units made a most gallant advance over the open unsupported by covering fire of any kind, but the Germans were by this time strongly entrenched in Neuve Chapelle, and the attack failed with heavy loss. After dark the Dorsets moved to the cover of farms at St. Vaast, about half a mile north of the day positions, and were there joined by the draft under Capt. Fraser. There was much heavy rifle fire during the night, but no hostile attack, and at 4.15 a.m. on the 29th the Dorsets moved back to billets at Rue de l'Epinette, being still under the commander of the 14th Brigade. Efforts were made to reorganise and absorb the new draft, but they were hampered by the frequent calls made upon the battalion to go to the support of units in the line. An order to be in readiness to support the 2nd Manchesters at La Quinque Rue was cancelled at 9.30 a.m., but orders to send two companies away arrived at 11 a.m., and " A " and " B " set off for Rue de Bethune, there to come under the 13th Brigade. They were not, however, employed in any fighting, though they suffered casualties from shell-fire. They returned to Rue de l'Epinette at 6.30 p.m.

The 29th October proved to be the last day the Dorsets spent in this area. The relief of the IInd Corps by the Indian Corps was about to commence. But it was a lively day in the La Quinque Rue sector. The Germans made two determined attacks upon the 2nd Manchesters, but they were repulsed. All through the afternoon troops of the Indian Corps were moving up towards the front. It was a dismal day of leaden skies and pouring rain—an unhappy beginning for the native troops. That night the relief commenced in earnest,

X

THE MOVE TO THE MESSINES FRONT

(See Map H)

A sudden move by 'bus—The Messines Front—A sixteen-days' spell in
the line—Major Saunders wounded—Dranoutre—The first winter
of trench warfare.

THE long-desired orders for the departure of the Dorsets
arrived during the morning of the 30th October, another
pouring wet day, and at 2 p.m. they set out on a 12-mile
march to their new billets at Calonne-sur-la-Lys, moving
by Locon. All ranks were heartily glad to say good-bye
to the Givenchy–Festubert area, with its sodden fields
and heavy fighting, for the battalion had suffered terribly
there and had had no opportunity of that rest and
reorganisation which later years showed to be essential
after a spell of heavy fighting.

The period ending on the 30th October has been described in some detail, for though it is realised that the
Dorsets took part in no action of real importance after
the battle of the 13th, it is necessary to understand how
great a strain was imposed on all ranks during that time,
and to show how thin was the line at all points. Much
has been written elsewhere of the hardships suffered by
those troops who fought at Ypres in October, 1914. Let
it never be forgotten that an equally severe strain was
borne by the battalions of the IInd Corps in their attempt,
first to outflank the hostile northern wing, and later,
when thrown on the defensive, to resist, day and night,
the repeated attempts of the enemy to press through to
Bethune.

Calonne-sur-la-Lys was an unattractive village, but it
had one compensation—an entire freedom from shells.
All through the night of the 30th/31st the distant rumble
of guns could be heard towards the north.

The 31st October—the most critical day on the Ypres
front—was fine, and the Dorsets marched in comfort
the 13 miles to their billets at Strazeele. There were
now prospects of several days' rest, but they were rudely
dispelled at 7 a.m. on the 1st November by the arrival
of Col. Shoubridge of the IInd Corps Staff (who spent his

early soldiering days in the 39th), with orders that the
battalion was to be ready to move at once by 'bus to
Wulverghem. The 'buses arrived in the village at 10
a.m., and while they were being loaded the Corps Commander, Sir Horace Smith-Dorrien, addressed the officers.
He spoke in very complimentary terms of the work the
battalion had done since Mons, with special reference to
their fine fighting at Pont Fixe, and explained that the
Germans were pressing the 4th Division at Ploegsteert,
and that Messines had been lost. He said he had specially
selected the Dorsets as one of the two battalions to be
sent to help the 4th Division.

At 10.15 a.m. the 'bus column started. The 'buses
still contained the advertisements with which they had
been decorated when following their normal routine in
London. The journey was pleasant enough. It was a
glorious autumn day, and the country was quite untouched by war. The 'bus column proceeded via Bailleul–
Dranoutre–Lindenhoek to Neuve Eglise, where the
Dorsets formed up in a field. While passing Lindenhoek
heavy shelling could be seen at Wytschaete, which had
now passed into German hands. At 3.30 p.m. the
Dorsets were moved into billets at Neuve Eglise, but at
5 p.m. " B," " C," and " D " Companies were ordered
out to entrench a line south of and astride the Neuve
Eglise–Wulverghem Road, about half a mile east of the
former village. Later all were withdrawn, except one
platoon of " B " Company left to block the road. The
night passed quietly, and at 2 p.m. on the 2nd November
the Dorsets were ordered to a supporting position in
Ploegsteert Wood.

As the Germans were maintaining continuous pressure
upon the 4th Division line on the front Le Gheer–St.
Yves, " A " Company was ordered to move up in support
in the wood about half a mile east of the former village,
while " B " and " D " were sent to entrench a line along
one of the rides of the wood about half a mile further
back. During the morning and afternoon of the 3rd
November companies remained as stated, but at 6 p.m.
they commenced to relieve the 1st Royal Irish Fusiliers
in incomplete trenches with " C " Company astride the
Ploegsteert–Messines Road, and the front continued by
" A," " B," and " D " Companies, the flank of the latter
resting on the River Douve. The battalion thus covered

two important tactical features—the Messines Road and Hill 63.

It is not proposed to describe in detail the days spent in this sector. They numbered sixteen without relief. The Germans became more aggressive daily and shelled certain areas heavily day and night. The front was a long one, and touch on the Douve flank was always difficult to maintain, as for days the French were operating in that neighbourhood in their efforts to recapture Messines, and by the nature of their tactics their front was somewhat " fluid."

About 7 p.m. on the 5th November a heavy outburst of fire astride the Messines Road was followed by reports that a hostile attack had penetrated the line there ; necessary precautions were taken at once, but it proved to be a false alarm. On the 7th November warning was received that a general hostile attack was expected, but the Germans made no sign. On the 14th Major Saunders decided to move his headquarters from the trench on the lower north-eastern slopes of Hill 63 to the château lodge near the road. The Headquarters' trench had been " spotted " by the enemy, who had been making very accurate shooting with 5·9 howitzers without actually getting a direct hit. During the stay of Headquarters in this trench Pte. Coombes, a signaller, was wounded in the chest when carrying a message from Brigade Head-quarters, but notwithstanding that a lung had been penetrated he completed his mission. He was deseevedly awarded a D.C.M.

But the change of headquarters brought with it bad luck, for Major Saunders, while taking his morning walk to visit companies, received a shell wound in the foot and had to be evacuated. From the day on which Col. Bols had been wounded Major Saunders had commanded the battalion in a manner which maintained in all ranks a feeling of quiet confidence. Major Saunders never spared himself, and his active brain was constantly at work preparing for all eventualities. He had many difficulties to face—heavy losses, lack of opportunities for reorganisation, rapidly changing situations, new officers—but he never failed to produce a sound solution for every problem. His loss, for his wound proved to be most troublesome, was in the nature of a disaster.

On the following day Capt. Williams assumed command

of the battalion, as Major Fraser was temporarily absent as Brigade Transport Officer. On the 16th November a readjustment of the front enabled " C " and " D " companies to be withdrawn from the line. That afternoon " B " Company, now in trenches near the Messines Road, were heavily shelled by 8-inch and 5·9-inch shells, and a number of men were buried.

The 17th and 18th November were spent chiefly in digging, but during the night of the 18th/19th the Dorsets were at last finally relieved by the 1st Royal Irish Fusiliers, and in the early hours of the 19th companies had concentrated at Petit Pont. At 7 a.m. the battalion, by this time quite worn out, marched to Dranoutre and took up billets in farms south and south-east of that village. Major Fraser returned to command the battalion, which now came under the orders of Brig.-Gen. Maude, commanding the 14th Brigade. It should be explained here that the 15th Brigade was scattered at this period. Brig.-Gen. Count Gleichen, with the Bedfords and the Cheshires, was near Hooge, east of Ypres. The remaining battalion, the Norfolks, was at Laventie, helping the Indian Corps.

The Dorsets remained at Dranoutre until the 24th November. On the 21st November Gen. Sir Horace Smith-Dorrien paid an informal visit to Battalion Headquarters and expressed a wish to see the Dorsets on parade the following day. This he did the next afternoon and addressed the battalion at some length and in very complimentary terms.

The weather, which had been damp and mild, became more wintry on the eve of the battalion's return to the trenches. Snow fell, and a hard frost set in. On the evening of the 24th the Dorsets set out to relieve the 1st East Surreys in the sector west of Hill 75. There they remained until the 30th, when the 2nd Royal Scots Fusiliers relieved them, and they returned to Dranoutre.

The Hill 75 sector was distinctly lively. Hostile snipers were very active, for the German trenches being on higher ground commanded our own. The rifle fire at night was incessant and sometimes rose to a roar on both sides. As a result ration parties, reliefs, and runners suffered greatly from unaimed bullets during the hours of darkness. But these conditions, though unpleasantly novel in October, 1914, were encountered night after

night for months to come, until the climax was reached
at Ypres in March, 1915. Near the close of November
Capt. Williams left the battalion to take up an appointment at the Officer Cadet School which was being set up
at Bailleul. Capt. Williams' departure left only four of
those officers who sailed from Belfast with the battalion
—Major Fraser (commanding), Capt. Ransome (adjutant),
Lieut. Partridge (Transport Officer), and 2/Lieut Shannon.

Capt. Williams' untimely death in April, 1915, from
pneumonia was a great loss to the regiment. His distinguished conduct at Wasmes on the 24th August, 1914,
was rewarded in February, 1915, with a Brevet Majority.

The months that followed found the Army settling
down to a long period of trench warfare. Trench warfare
is necessarily uninteresting and devoid of incident, and
it is not proposed to deal in detail with the winter months
of 1914–1915. The Dorsets during these months held
various sectors of trenches in front of Wulverghem, with
periods of rest at Neuve Eglise and Dranoutre, and later
on spent a few spells of eight days at Bailleul, at that
time a prosperous town quite untouched by war.

A word as to the trenches themselves. They consisted
chiefly of short lengths of breastwork, or trench, where
digging did not produce water two feet below the surface
of the ground. The men lived in the fire trench, there
being no dug-outs in these days, gaining what shelter
they could from the weather by means of hurdles placed
over the trenches. Support trenches were few in number,
supports, reserves, and Battalion Headquarters being
accommodated in ruined farms which were scattered
liberally over the country-side. Barbed wire in front of
the trench line was practically non-existent.

After the brief cold spell at the end of November the
weather was generally mild and wet. The mud was
indescribable. Not only the trenches themselves, but all
tracks leading to them soon became well-nigh impassable.
Trenches had frequently to be abandoned altogether
owing to their water-logged condition, and new ones, or
rather breastworks, constructed.

Fortunately the enemy was unusually quiet. He
contented himself with " sniping," at which he was very
adept, obtaining many victims among our men. His
guns were active on our batteries by day—he seldom, if
ever, fired at night—but he seemed generally to refrain

from shelling the numerous occupied farms, unless he observed any movement. Doubtless he did not wish to encourage our guns to retaliate on the farms on his side of the line.

At this period our artillery was deplorably short of ammunition, and such shells as were available were practically all shrapnel. The Germans when they liked could bombard any area with high explosive shells from their 15 cm. howitzers.

Christmas, 1914, was spent with two companies in the line and the rest of the Dorsets at Neuve Eglise. This was the occasion of the one and only Christmas " truce " during the war. Nothing unusual in this connection occurred on the Dorsets' front, except that no shot was fired by either side on Christmas Day, but further south a certain amount of "friendly " intercourse took place. At one point a British soldier is said to have shaved a German in " No Man's Land."

On the 12th December Major Walshe, South Staffordshire Regiment, assumed command of the battalion, vice Major Fraser, and retained command until the return of Lieut.-Col. Bols in January, 1915.

On the 24th February Lieut.-Col. Bols was appointed to the command of the 84th Brigade (28th Division), and Major Walshe resumed command of the Dorsets.

XI

THE YPRES SALIENT

(SEE MAP K)

The "Bluff" and the "International" trench—Unpleasant conditions—
Major Cowie assumes command—The battle of Hill 60 opens.

DURING the third week in February heavy gun-fire was
heard to the north of Wulverghem on two successive
nights, and it transpired that a hostile attack had taken
place at St. Eloi, where several trenches had been lost.
The St. Eloi front had only recently been taken over
from the French and was held by our 27th and 28th
Divisions. These divisions, which had only arrived from
England during January, consisted of British battalions
brought home from India and other stations in the tropics.
The men had had no time to become acclimatised, and
fever was very prevalent among them. The portion of
front they had taken over was a very unpleasant, and at
the same time a very important one, being the southern
bend of the Ypres salient. The situation south-east of
Ypres was therefore critical, and it was decided to replace
three brigades of the 27th and 28th Divisions by the 9th
Brigade (3rd Division) and the 13th and 15th Brigades
(5th Division). Consequently the Dorsets with the rest
of the 15th Brigade left Bailleul on the 3rd March, 1915,
and marching north by Locre–La Clytte–Ouderdom, went
into an uncomfortable hutment camp on the roadside
between Ouderdom and Vlamertinghe. On the 4th March
the Dorsets marched through Ypres to relieve the 1st
Lincolns north of the Ypres–Comines Canal, with their
right resting on the "Bluff." It was an unpleasant
relief. The Ypres–St. Eloi Road was shelled at several
points between the Lille Gate and the bend of the canal
by Lankhoff Château. The area leading from the road
to the front trenches was swept by bullets to an extent
that was distinctly abnormal. Both sides used their
rifles at night with great persistence, and the fact that the
fire was in a great measure unaimed led to the arrival of
bullets at all sorts of unexpected places. Many were the
casualties caused by these "strays," and the effect upon

E   65

the nerves became increasingly great amongst those who had to face these conditions night after night.

The Dorsets remained in this sector until the 16th March, sharing the front line in turn with the Bedfords, and when in support occupying Lankhoff Château and another white château on the Ypres–St. Eloi Road, the stables of which were dignified by the name " Bedford House " soon after the arrival of the 15th Brigade. The trenches in the sector were extremely poor. The parapets were in few places bullet-proof, and this may be realised more fully when it is remembered that the Dorsets suffered over 90 casualties from small-arms fire alone during their first tour of duty of six days.

The front contained two " tender spots "—the " Bluff," famous for many months to come as a scene of heavy fighting, and the " International " trench. The " Bluff " was a big spoil bank on the northern edge of the Ypres–Comines Canal, giving a good view of the German positions, but open to enfilade fire from hostile guns behind the Messines–Wytschaete Ridge. The " International " trench—numbered 32a—had originally been British, but during the confused fighting towards the end of February the southern half had been lost, so that it was occupied by Germans at the southern end and by British at the northern end, with two barricades in the centre. The trenches on this front were not continuous, nor sited in accordance with the shape of the ground. Only one support trench existed, and Battalion Headquarters and one company occupied a large red-roofed farm marked La Chapelle on the maps and in full view of Wytschaete village.

As has already been stated the enemy was distinctly more aggressive in this sector than he had been at Wulverghem. His " snipers " had the upper hand for some days, but gradually our men began to even matters.

Early on the 9th March a party of 30 or 40 Germans attempted to surprise the garrison of the " International " trench, consisting of 3 platoons of " D " Company. They were seen by the sentries and driven back to their own trench by rifle fire. The Brigade Commander hearing of this incident wired the message, " Well done, garrison of 32a," to Battalion Headquarters.

The Germans continued to show an anxiety to gain possession of the whole of the " International " trench, and during the 10th March, which was wet, they began to pump water into the British part of the trench and to breach the parapet with shells and trench-mortar bombs. On this day they also shelled the Headquarters farm for over three hours, and " B " Company had to be withdrawn from the barns to the open fields.

But the most important event of this period occurred about sunset on the 14th March. A relief of the Dorsets by the Bedfords had just commenced when a big explosion was observed south of the canal on the front of the 27th Division, followed immediately by a heavy hostile bombardment of the St. Eloi sector. It transpired that the Germans had exploded a mine under a mound in the 27th Division's front line and had launched an attack which gained a footing in several trenches.

Nothing unusual occurred north of the canal, however, and the relief progressed as ordered. But as soon as the Dorsets reached " Bedford House " after relief, " D " Company with two machine-guns, under 2/Lieut. Stanley-Clarke, was despatched to hold the canal bridge close to Lankhof Château. Early on the 15th March " A " Company was ordered forward to support " D " Company. For a long while the situation at St. Eloi remained obscure, though the enemy had undoubtedly penetrated into the village in small parties following on their initial attack. But counter-attacks by the 27th Division practically restored the situation, and it was possible to withdraw " A " and " D " Companies about 5.30 a.m., although two machine-guns remained to guard the canal bridge.

On the 16th March the Dorsets returned for six days to the Ouderdom huts, but the 21st March saw them back in the line again in relief of the 4th Royal Fusiliers (3rd Division), this time holding a sector further north than their previous one. This tour was uneventful, and the Dorsets were withdrawn on the 23rd March into Brigade Reserve in the Infantry Barracks in Ypres.

The town of Ypres was at this time quite habitable. Only the portion round the square in which the Cloth Hall stood, and the neighbourhood of the railway station, had been badly shelled. Many cafés and shops were open. A large market was held regularly, when the streets were thronged with peasants from the neighbouring villages. Any hostile shelling that took place was directed on the Cloth Hall and the Menin Gate.

After a spell in reserve a further tour of duty in the trenches followed, and the 31st March found the 15th Brigade back once more in the Ouderdom huts.

The first weeks of April, 1915, were quiet and uneventful, two spells in the line, broken by a couple of days in huts near Reninghelst, merely produced normal conditions of trench warfare.

Early in April Major Cowie assumed command of the battalion, vice Major Walshe who rejoined his own unit. Major Cowie had for several months been employed as Commandant of an Officers' Training School at Bailleul and had with great difficulty obtained permission to return to regimental duty.

The effect of Major Cowie's personality on all ranks of the battalion was most marked. Absolutely fearless, he would visit all parts of the front daily, never an easy matter in those days when trenches were not continuous and the approaches to them destitute of cover from view at many points. Some of the older men serving with the battalion at that time—men of Section " D " of the Army Reserve—had known Major Cowie in the Tirah Campaign of 1898, and he never failed to remember them. Major Cowie only held the command for a little over three weeks, but it is no exaggeration to say that the battalion advanced in moral and fighting efficiency in a very marked degree even in that short time.

The Dorsets at this period completely dominated the Germans opposite to them. Hostile " sniping " was reduced to a minimum, and any German sniper who became a nuisance was marked down and invariably dealt with successfully. A careful programme of machine-gun harassing fire was carried out every night, and a number of contrivances, calculated to annoy the enemy and reduce his moral, were invented and put into practice under the direction of Lieut. Morley. These were the days before the " Stokes Mortar " and the " Mills Bomb," but Lieut. Morley used an improvised mortar—in reality a stove pipe,—and even filled empty bottles with powder and nails and employed them as hand-grenades. Several patrolling excursions were successfully carried out by 2/Lieut. Wood who was unfortunately killed later when going out alone to a German trench.

For some weeks past the Higher Command had been planning an operation which was to have for its object

the capture of a small hill just north of the Ypres–
Comines Railway, known as Hill 60. Elaborate mining
operations had been in progress for some weeks, and it
was intended to explode six charges and then to rush the
hill under cover of the explosions. The 17th April was
the date fixed for this attack which was to be carried out
by the 13th Brigade.

XII

THE FIGHTING AT HILL 60

(SEE MAP L)

The Dorsets move to Hill 60—The first gas attack, 1st May, 1915—
2/Lieut. Kestell-Cornish holds the hill-top—His gallantry—The
situation well in hand—Heavy gas casualties—A pause in the
fighting—Major Cowie mortally wounded—The second gas attack,
5th May, 1915—A critical situation—The Dorsets' counter-attack
—Situation at nightfall—The Dorsets withdrawn—Further gas
casualties.

ON the 17th April the Dorsets held a sector from the
" Bluff " (exclusive) to a point a few hundred yards from
the Ypres–Comines Railway. Their orders for co-operation
in the attack upon Hill 60 were to open rifle and machine-
gun fire upon the hostile trenches opposite as soon as the
attack commenced. At 7 p.m. the mines were exploded,
which was the signal for a heavy bombardment by our
guns. Hostile retaliation followed almost at once, and
our trenches and the woods in rear of them were shelled.
Into details of the heavy fighting which took place on
Hill 60 from this date until the 29th April it is not
proposed to enter. Suffice it to say that on the latter
date the hill was in British hands, though the Germans
had made repeated attempts to retake it and had
succeeded more than once, only to be ejected again. But
the fighting was incessant, the hostile shelling very
severe, and the losses on both sides enormous. By the
29th April no fewer than nine different battalions had
been employed in the fighting on this very narrow front.

But the fighting on the hill had also been the cause of
increased hostile shelling on both flanks. During the
evening of the 20th a hostile bombardment of " C "
Company's front resulted in some 30 casualties, including
Capt. Thwaytes, its commander, and two other officers
wounded ; and this bombardment was repeated on the
following evening.

At 6.30 p.m. on the 22nd April very heavy hostile
shelling broke out towards the north, coupled with a
bombardment of Ypres and its eastern exits. Enormous
shells, said to be fired from a 42-cm. howitzer, began to
fall in Ypres at intervals of fifteen minutes. That some-

70

thing more than an exhibition of hatred was intended was soon proved by the cancellation of the relief fixed for the same evening. This bombardment was, in fact, the opening of the Second Battle of Ypres, when the Germans, employing poison gas for the first time, sought to break through between the Canadians and the French about Langemarck.

The battle continued to rage towards the north-east of Ypres, and orders to reconnoitre positions along the canal between Ypres and Lankhof Château, in case a retirement became necessary, pointed to the gravity of the situation. Secret preparatory orders were actually issued to companies for use in the event of such a withdrawal being ordered. But no such orders were issued, and on the 25th April the Dorsets were relieved and withdrawn to Kruisstraat, a suburb of Ypres. At this time Ypres was under continual heavy bombardment, and the incessant din of bursting shells rendered sleep out of the question. Major Cowie, therefore, obtained permission to move the Dorsets into bivouac to the south of Kruisstraat. For two days each company was employed in digging a new line known as "The Hooge Switch," for occupation in case the front had to be readjusted owing to events further north.

As the Dorsets were now in reserve, and the heavy fighting still continued on Hill 60, it came as no surprise when orders arrived on the 29th April that they were that evening to relieve the 2nd Camerons who were in close support of the 1st Devons holding the actual hill-top. The approach to the front line was an unpleasant experience. The Germans were employing a very thorough programme of harassing fire. The canal bridges, all roads and tracks, and finally the railway cutting leading to Hill 60 were under incessant shell-fire. The support position consisted of shelters dug into the hill-side and covered with corrugated iron and sandbags.

At 3 p.m., 30th April, the Dorsets relieved the Devons in the trenches, the latter going into support. When the relief was complete the Dorsets had "A," "C," and "D" Companies in the front line—"C" Company holding the trench on the crest of the hill—and "B" Company in support.

The 1st May was a fine sunny day with a very slight south-easterly breeze. Nothing of importance occurred, indeed the enemy was unusually quiet. At 7 p.m., however, the enemy commenced a bombardment of the sector, and it soon became evident that something unusual was in progress. The first news of the presence of gas was a telephonic message from Capt. Hawkins, whose company, "D," was holding the left portion of the front, known as the Zwarteleen Salient. He described the situation as serious and expressed a doubt as to his ability to hold his trenches owing to the gas. It appeared that at 7.15 p.m. the enemy had discharged gas from at least five points in their front line—three opposite the right trench, No. 38, and two in front of the Zwarteleen Salient. The breeze carried the gas to the left of No. 38 trench, garrisoned by "A" Company, but Hill 60 trench and the salient were seriously affected. The Hill 60 trench was garrisoned by one platoon of "C" Company under command of 2/Lieut. Kestell-Cornish. Many of the men were overcome, but 2/Lieut. Kestell-Cornish and four privates remained at their posts, though all were badly affected by the gas. They opened a rapid fire to their front, moving to different points in the trench in turn. Whether the Germans had intended to attack in force is uncertain, but there seems no reason to doubt that strong patrols at least approached the trench, while bombing parties assailed its flanks, moving down the old communication trenches leading into it. 2/Lieut. Kestell-Cornish and his four assistants by their gallantry and remarkable devotion to duty in circumstances then without parallel in civilised warfare, undoubtedly made it clear to the assailants that the gas had not done its work completely. In any case the enemy made no sign, beyond persistently bombing the flanks of the trench. But, notwithstanding the gallant stand by the remnants of the garrison of the hill, the situation was still very serious. At this juncture Capt. Batten, commanding "B" Company, acted with great promptitude. He despatched supports to the aid of "D" Company, and himself went forward to the hill-top with a platoon. By this time 2/Lieut. Kestell-Cornish and his men had been overcome by the gas, so that Capt. Batten's arrival was most timely. Meanwhile the O.C. Devons had ordered up two of his companies which took over the Zwarteleen Salient and its support line. Major Cowie, accompanied by the Adjutant, had already proceeded to the hill and assumed command there. He found that Capt. Batten had made excellent dispositions and that the situation was quiet, except for intermittent hostile bombing. He then went to the salient, now garrisoned by the Devons, and found the extremely deep and narrow trenches blocked with dead, with many others dying in terrible agony. It was a deplorable sight and one which no eye-witness can ever forget. A visit to " A " Company on the right followed. This company had escaped the gas and was intact. By 10 p.m. the situation had become practically normal, and Major Cowie returned to his headquarters in the railway cutting.

An examination of the casualty returns brought to light the terrible ravages caused by the gas. They showed 2/Lieut. Butcher and 52 other ranks dead, and in addition the following were admitted to the Field Ambulance suffering from gas poisoning : Capt. Hawkins, 2/Lieut. Sampson, 2/Lieut. Roberts (afterwards died), 2/Lieut. Hodgson, 2/Lieut. Weston-Stevens, and 200 other ranks. Many of these 200 men succumbed subsequently. In addition 32 other ranks were missing, men who had crawled away to die, and whose bodies were located afterwards. Only one man was killed and one wounded by rifle or shell-fire.

2/Lieut. Kestell-Cornish was sent to hospital two days later, suffering from the effects of gas, but was able to return to duty in a week's time, having flatly refused to be sent to England in accordance with medical advice. This gallant young officer, through whose devotion to duty and presence of mind the battalion front had been kept intact, and Hill 60, which had already cost so many lives, maintained in British hands, was shortly afterwards awarded the Military Cross. Immediate rewards were not authorised in those days, but Sir John French, on hearing the facts, made the award as a special case. It is not too much to say that the Victoria Cross would have been a fitting reward in the abnormal and demoralising circumstances existing at the time of the act. After serving as Acting-Adjutant for some six months, 2/Lieut. Kestell-Cornish commanded " A " Company with distinction during the Somme battles in 1916, when he was wounded, and in 1917, and gained a bar to the Military Cross. In 1917 he was appointed Adjutant, and later became G.S.O. 3 of the 32nd Division. While holding that appointment he was mortally wounded in February, 1918, when reconnoitring during a heavy hostile attack.

It is well to remember that this first experience of a gas attack found the British troops practically un-protected against the fumes. A few pads of cotton-wool —quite insufficient in number—supplemented by some pieces of cloth, similar to tailor's patterns of lounge suitings, were totally inadequate to meet the case.

In describing the fighting on this day Sir John French, in a despatch dated 15th June, 1915, wrote : " On the 1st May another attempt to recapture Hill 60 was supported by great volumes of asphyxiating gas which caused nearly all the men along a front of 400 yards to be immediately struck down by its fumes. The splendid courage with which the leaders rallied their men and subdued the natural tendency to panic (which is inevitable on such occasions), combined with the prompt inter-vention of supports, once more drove the enemy back."

On the 2nd May the Devons once more took over the front line, and the Dorsets went back into support. On the 4th May the Duke of Wellingtons, 800 strong, relieved the Devons, and Major Cowie assumed command of the troops in the sector. Early on the 5th May a great misfortune overtook the Dorsets. Major Cowie, who had just returned about 5.45 a.m. from a visit to the front line, was hit by a fragment of shell and dangerously wounded. The shell was a stray one which pitched at the entrance to the Aid Post, close by the Headquarters' dug-out. Major Cowie died of wounds some days later, and thus the Dorset Regiment sustained its heaviest loss in the whole war.

The command of the Dorsets now devolved upon Capt. Ransome, while 2/Lieut. Morris was appointed to act as Adjutant.

At 9 a.m. a message, " gas coming over," was tele-phoned from the front line, and simultaneously a con-siderable number of troops could be seen retiring along the railway line. " C " and " D " Companies, very weak in numbers after their numerous " gas " casualties on the 1st, were ordered forward at once to support the Duke of Wellingtons. As a stream of gassed and demoralised men continued to pour down the railway line, " A " and " B " Companies were ordered forward ten minutes later. By this time all the telephone lines both to the front and rear had been cut by the hostile bombardment, and the gas was very thick even at Battalion Headquarters. When at length the telephone line to 38 trench had been repaired, information came in which showed the situation to be as follows : The Germans were holding Hill 60, portions of 39 and 40 trenches, and the Zwarteleen Salient. The Duke of Wellingtons had been badly gassed, and " A," " B," and " C " Companies were holding 38 trench and the greater part of 39 trench.

This indicated a very serious situation indeed, for the portion of front still in British hands was a very minor part of the whole. There seemed to be nothing, either in the shape of troops or trenches, to prevent the enemy from pressing on into Ypres itself. And at about 11 a.m. it appeared as if this appreciation of the situation would indeed prove correct, for parties of Germans had begun to infiltrate towards Zillebeke. To meet this menacing situation the details of Battalion Headquarters, supplemented by men already partially gassed, were placed to cover the gap, in positions from which they could bring fire to bear towards the north. To add to the gravity of the situation repeated messages came in from the front line to say that our shells were falling short.

The telephone line to Brigade Headquarters having at length been repaired, a message arrived to say that the Cheshires were on their way to Hill 60, and that their Commanding Officer (Lieut.-Col. Scott) would take over command of all the troops in the neighbourhood. Lieut.-Col. Scott went forward to reconnoitre, but was almost immediately killed by an unseen rifleman, and Major Hughes of the Cheshires assumed command. The Cheshires advanced against the enemy in the Zwarteleen Salient, dealing effectively with the party of Germans who had penetrated as far as Zillebeke. By 1 p.m. the Cheshires had made good progress, but were unable to eject the enemy from the trenches he had won.

Meanwhile the Dorsets, reinforced by a party of Cheshires, recaptured 39 trench and made good progress along 40 trench by means of bombing attacks. 2/Lieut. Shannon and 2/Lieut. Mansel-Pleydell displayed great bravery and initiative in the confused fighting which raged on the hill-side all the afternoon. 2/Lieut. Shannon was killed and 2/Lieut. Mansel-Pleydell wounded in the head, though not seriously. Capt. Lilly had the misfortune to be wounded in 38 trench by one of our own 4·7 shells about 1 p.m. At dusk the situation in the sector was as follows : The Dorsets and the Cheshires held 38 and 39 trenches and the greater part of 40 trench, while the Germans were still in occupation of the crest of Hill 60 and of the Zwarteleen Salient, faced by the Cheshires and the 6th Liverpools who were digging in opposite.

Counter-attacks launched by two battalions of the 13th Brigade at 10 p.m. failed to make any progress owing to the darkness of the night, the difficulties of previous reconnaissance, and the impossibility of affording adequate artillery support.

At 2 a.m. on the 6th May the Dorsets were withdrawn to their old bivouac near Kruisstraat, when an examination of company rolls revealed the fact that the battalion which had gone into the line on the 30th April over 800 strong now numbered 173 all ranks. Of the survivors, including officers, all were more or less affected by gas and worn out by incessant fighting and anxiety.

The casualties sustained on the 5th May were : 2/Lieut. Shannon and 14 other ranks killed. Major Cowie, Capt. Lilly, and 2/Lieut. Morley and 48 other ranks wounded. Capt. Batten, 2/Lieut. Stanley-Clarke, 2/Lieut. Sigrist, and 60 other ranks gassed. 2/Lieut. Bosley and 48 other ranks missing. Total—8 officers and 160 other ranks.

XIII

REST AND REORGANISATION

(See Map L)

The Dorsets reorganised with large reinforcements of officers and men
—The youth and inexperience of the former—Back to Hill 60—
Trench warfare.

At 8 p.m. on the 6th May the Dorsets marched to the
Ouderdom huts, where they remained till the evening of
20th May. During this period several large drafts arrived
and in addition nearly 20 officers, all except one being
2/Lieutenants. Everything possible was done to reorganise the battalion, but many of the officers were
quite without Army experience, and few of the old and
tried N.C.O.'s remained. Companies were allotted as
follows : " A " Company : 2/Lieut. Mansel-Pleydell,
3rd Dorsets. " B " Company : Lieut. Moutray, Royal
Inniskilling Fusiliers. " C " Company : 2/Lieut. Earle,
3rd Dorsets. " D " Company : Capt. Crankshaw, 3rd
Dorsets.

2/Lieut. Kestell-Cornish, having recovered from the
effects of the gas, took over the duties of Acting-Adjutant,
while 2/Lieut. Morris was appointed Machine-Gun Officer.
Capt. Ransome remained in command.

On the 20th May news arrived that the Dorsets were
to return to Hill 60 once more, and they set out about
8 p.m. nearly 1100 strong to relieve the 1st Gordons. By
1 a.m., 21st May, this relief was effected without the
slightest hitch, which speaks well for the care and initiative displayed by the youthful Company Commanders.
The Gordons were thoroughly helpful and made excellent
arrangements for the relief.

The Dorsets found themselves holding the following
trenches : 38, 39, 41, 41a (a new fire-trench dug by the
Gordons in front of 41), 42, and 47 support. The enemy
still held the crest of Hill 60, the Zwarteleen Salient, and
the greater part of 40 trench. There followed an anxious
tour of duty, for the inexperience of all ranks could not
be forgotten, and the possibility of further hostile attacks
had always to be reckoned with. But the Germans remained fairly quiet, content no doubt with the view of

the surrounding country which the crest of Hill 60
afforded.   But their snipers were active, and they
persisted in breaching the parapet of 38 trench almost
daily.   In these circumstances the spirit and initiative
of all ranks were beyond praise.   Several daring patrols
were carried out, and in this connection 2/Lieut. Agalasto
did excellent work.   Throughout this tour of duty the
Brigade Commander (Brig.-Gen. Northey) visited the
Dorsets every day, and by his sympathy and advice did
much to encourage the troops and increase their moral.
It may be noted here that the excellent patrol work done
by the Dorsets during this period was referred to by Sir
John French in his despatch of the 15th October, 1915.

On the 1st June the Dorsets were withdrawn into
Brigade Reserve in dug-outs along the railway close to
Brigade Headquarters, where they remained until the
13th June.   Another spell in the Hill 60 sector followed,
which was uneventful, although more good patrol and
other work was accomplished.   The 17th June found the
Dorsets once more in Brigade Reserve in the railway
dug-outs.

XIV

CONCLUSION

Services of Lieut. and Q.M. Alderman and R.S.M. Pell—The Machine-Gun Section—Lessons.

IT is impossible to close this narrative without a reference to the valuable services rendered by the undermentioned individuals :

Lieut. and Quartermaster W. Alderman took over his duties in November, 1914, at Ploegsteert Wood. From that time forward his efficiency, initiative, and enthusiasm were unbounded. No battalion could have been better served by its Quartermaster, and it was not only in the performance of his duties that he excelled. His knowledge, experience, and advice were of the utmost value during periods of reorganisation—for example, during the period outlined at the close of the narrative.

R.S.M. J. Pell served throughout the period covered by this narrative with a zeal and ability which could not fail to leave its mark. Throughout the retreat from Mons he rendered valuable assistance to the Quartermaster and transport officer in addition to his normal duties. He acted as Quartermaster for a period after the departure of Major Kearney, always with success, and at a later date officiated as Transport Officer, when an officer could not be spared to perform this duty. The effect of his strong personality, both in peace and war, will not be forgotten.

In this short account of the doings of the Dorsets in France and Belgium in the first ten months of the Great War it has not been possible, however desirable it may seem, to mention by name more than two or three N.C.O.'s or men who performed specific acts of gallantry. The names of those whose conduct was brought to notice are contained in Appendix C; and there were doubtless many more whose deeds in the turmoil of active operations escaped the notice they deserve. But in war this must ever be so.

But a final reference must be made to that most efficient little unit, the Machine-Gun Section. Trained with care and enthusiasm by Lieut. Algeo before the outbreak of war, and led with skill and dash by Lieut. Woodhouse in the early months of the fighting, the section by its fine fighting spirit, high standard of efficiency, and excellent comradeship, distinguished itself on all occasions on which it was called into play.

In the defence of Troisvilles on the afternoon of the 26th August, 1914, in the heavy fighting near Givenchy on the 12th and 13th October, 1914, and in face of the gas-cloud at Hill 60 on the 1st May, 1915, it covered itself with glory. Many of the older hands lost their lives on this latter day, notably Sergt. Gambling, who was discovered lying on the parapet beside his gun which he had worked to the last. The award of the Distinguished Conduct Medal, for which honour he had been recommended in recognition of his fine services in October, 1914, was not gazetted until after his death.

Finally, what are the military lessons to be derived from a study of this early period of the Great War ? They are many, but three are of outstanding importance.

Firstly, the value of march discipline, without which even the deployment on the Mons Canal would have been seriously hampered, while the successful and ordered retreat of some 180 miles to the gates of Paris, followed by the victorious advance to Aisne, would have been impossible of achievement. In peace time the Dorsets had always prided themselves on their marching powers, and justly so, and no effort however exacting seemed to be beyond their powers, as the survivors of those who covered the 37 miles from Belfast to Ballykinlar in May, 1914, may recall. History has proved that the trouble expended then and earlier was amply repaid.

Secondly, the need of a high standard of musketry efficiency, which factor, perhaps more than any other, took the sting out of the German hordes at the very outset.

And lastly, the possession of true discipline, that discipline which is the fruit of the good comradeship and of mutual respect between officers and men in times of peace.

APPENDICES

APPENDIX A

Battalion Headquarters.
Commanding : Lieut.-Col. L. J. Bols, D.S.O.
Senior Major : Major R. T. Roper.
Adjutant : Capt. A. L. Ransome.
Quartermaster : Major J. Kearney.
Transport Officer : Lieut. C. F. M. Margetts.

" A " Company.
Commanding : Capt. W. A. C. Fraser.
2nd in Command : Capt. R. G. B. Maxwell-Hyslop.[1]

Platoon Commanders : Lieut. J. M. Pitt, Lieut. C. O. Lilly,
2/Lieut. F. D. S. King (3rd Battalion), 2/Lieut. G. S.
Shannon (Supplementary List).

" B " Company.
Commanding : Capt. H. S. Williams.
Platoon Commanders : Lieut. J. R. Turner (3rd Battalion),
Lieut. C. G. Butcher.

" C " Company.
Commanding : Major C. Saunders.
2nd in Command : Capt. J. Kelsall.
Platoon Commanders : Lieut. A. S. Fraser, Lieut. L.
Grant-Dalton, Lieut. W. A. Leishman, 2/Lieut. G. A.
Burnand (3rd Battalion).

" D " Company.
Commanding : Capt. W. T. C. Davidson.
2nd in Command : Capt. F. H. B. Rathborne.
Platoon Commanders : Lieut. R. E. Partridge, Lieut.
A. K. D. George, Lieut. A. E. Hawkins.
Machine-Gun Officer: Lieut. C. H. Woodhouse.

With H.Q. 15th Infantry Brigade.
Staff-Captain : Capt. A. L. Moulton-Barrett.
Brigade Machine-Gun Officer : Capt. A. R. M. Roe.

[1] Proceeded to France in advance of the battalion as Brigade
Billeting Officer.

APPENDIX B

ROLL OF COMMANDING OFFICERS, ADJUTANTS, COMPANY
COMMANDERS, ETC., AUGUST, 1914, TO MAY, 1915

Commanding Officers :

Lieut.-Col. L. J. Bols, D.S.O.
Major C. Saunders.
Capt. H. S. Williams.
Major W. A. C. Fraser.
Major H. E. Walshe (South
Staffordshire Regiment).

Lieut.-Col. L. J. Bols, C.B.,
D.S.O.
Major H. E. Walshe (South
Staffordshire Regiment).
Major H. N. R. Cowie, D.S.O.
Capt. A. L. Ransome, M.C.

Adjutants :

Capt. A. L. Ransome.
Lieut. J. M. Pitt.
Capt. A. L. Ransome.

2/Lieut. C. H. Morris.
2/Lieut. R. V. Kestell-
Cornish, M.C.

Company Commanders :

"A" Company

Capt. Fraser.
Capt. Twiss (Indian Army).
Capt. Lloyd-Mostyn (Royal
Welch Fusiliers).
Capt. Lilly.
2/Lieut. Mansell-Pleydell
(3rd Battalion).

" B " Company

Capt. Williams.
Capt. Roe.
Capt. Kitchin.
Capt. Williams.
Capt. Codrington (Reserve of
Officers).
Capt. Batten (3rd Battalion).
Lieut. Moutray (R. Innis-
killing Fusiliers).

" C " Company

Major Saunders.
Capt. Kelsall.
Capt. Evans (S.W. Borderers).
Capt. Thwaytes.
Lieut. Butcher.
2/Lieut. Shannon.
2/Lieut. Earle (3rd Battalion).

" D " Company

Capt. Davidson.
Capt. Browne-Poole (3rd
Battalion).
Capt. Partridge.
Capt. Hawkins.
Capt. Crankshaw (3rd
Battalion).

Quartermasters :

Major J. Kearney.   Lieut. W. Alderman.

Machine-Gun Officers :

Lieut. Woodhouse.
Capt. Ransome.
Lieut. Woodhouse.

2/Lieut. Edmonds.
2/Lieut. Stanley-Clarke
2/Lieut. Morris.

Transport Officers :

Lieut. C. F. M. Margetts. | Lieut. R. E. Partridge.
2/Lieut. J. D. P. P. Stayner.

NOTE.—Names are arranged in the order in which officers actually performed duties. Actual dates of assumption and relinquishment of duties are not available.

APPENDIX C

HONOURS, AWARDS, AND MENTIONS IN DESPATCHES, AUGUST, 1914, TO JUNE, 1915.

Honours and Awards :

C.B.
Lieut.-Col. L. J. Bols, D.S.O.

C.M.G.
Major H. N. R. Cowie, D.S.O.
Major H. E. Walshe, S. Staffordshire Regiment (while com
manding 1st Dorset Regiment).

Brevet Majority.
Capt. H. S. Williams.

D.S.O.
Major C. Saunders. | Lieut. C. F. M. Margetts.
Lieut. C. O. Lilly.

Military Cross.
Capt. A. L. Ransome. | 2/Lieut. R. V. Kestell-Cornish
Lieut. R. E. Partridge. | (Immediate reward).
Lieut. C. H. Woodhouse. | 2/Lieut. F. J. Morley.
2/Lieut. G. S. Shannon. | R.S.M. J. Pell.

D.C.M.
C.S.M. Vivian. | Sergt. Gambling
Sergt. Creech. | Pte. Coombes.
Sergt. Snashall.

French " Croix-de-Guerre."

Capt. R. G. B. Maxwell-Hyslop.

Note.—The above only include the names of those awarded honours up to and including the *Gazette* of 3rd June, 1915. A number of other honours were gained for good work during the period August, 1914, to June, 1915, but these were gazetted at a later date.

Mentions in Despatches.

Lieut.-Col. L. J. Bols, D.S.O. (twice).
Major R. T. Roper.
Major H. N. R. Cowie, D.S.O.
Major C. Saunders.
Major W. A. C. Fraser.
Capt. H. S. Williams.
Capt. A. R. M. Roe.
Capt. A. L. Ransome (twice).
Capt. F. H. B. Rathborne.
Capt. R. E. Partridge.
Capt. A. E. Hawkins.
Capt. H. C. C. Batten (3rd Battalion).
Capt. E. K. Twiss (Indian Army—attached).
Major H. E. Walshe (South Staffordshire Regiment—attached).
Lieut. C. F. Margetts.
Lieut. C. H. Woodhouse.
Lieut. C. O. Lilly.
Lieut. R. V. Kestell-Cornish (3rd Battalion).
Lieut. C. G. Butcher.
Lieut. J. G. Clayton (3rd Battalion).

2/Lieut. G. S. Shannon.
2/Lieut. F. J. Morley.
2/Lieut. E. D. Le Sauvage.
2/Lieut. C. H. Morris.
Lieut. and Q.M. W. Alderman.
3537 R.S.M. J. Pell.
5622 Sergt. E. A. Hill.
6702 Sergt. A. Boater.
7587 Sergt. C. Gambling.
7773 Cpl. W. J. Cannings (twice).
8705 Cpl. W. Kerr (twice).
9302 L/Cpl. B. Laurence.
8831 L/Cpl. O. V. Ball.
8410 L/Cpl. R. Gough.
5860 Drummer W. Astridge.
6438 Drummer W. Prowse.
9246 Pte. T. A. Skipsey.
9322 Pte. R. Gent.
9226 Pte. W. Shonfield.
9129 Pte. F. J. Iles.
7461 Pte. W. H. Curtis.
4843 Pte. W. Dolman.
8053 Pte. F. W. Inker.
9037 Pte. F. Wheatcroft.
9290 Pte. H. J. Catalinet.
6749 Pte. W. Handley.

APPENDIX D

SUMMARY OF BATTLE CASUALTIES 23RD AUGUST, 1914, TO 15TH JUNE, 1915.

Date. 1914	OFFICERS.			OTHER RANKS.			Place.
	Killed.	Wounded.	Missing.	Killed.	Wounded.	Missing.	
23–24 Aug.	—	3	—	12	49	69	Battle of Mons.
26 Aug.	—	—	—	7	14	21	Battle of Le Cateau.
9 Sept.	—	4	—	7	31	4	Passage of the River Marne.
14–15 Sept.	—	—	—	2	41	4	Aisne.
12 Oct.	1	1	—	11	30	2	Pont Fixe.
13 Oct.	5	4	3	51	152	210	Pont Fixe.
14–21 Oct.	—	—	—	—	4	—	Festubert.
22 Oct.	—	3	1	7	22	101	Violaines.
29 Oct.	—	—	—	—	3	—	Festubert.
3–19 Nov.	—	1	—	8	20	1	Ploegsteert Wood.
24 Nov.–10 Dec.	1	—	—	1	16	1	Lindenhoek (trench warfare).
18–31 Dec.	—	—	—	4	18	—	Wulverghem (trench warfare).
1915.							
26 Jan.–23 Feb.	—	—	—	9	31	—	Wulverghem (trench warfare).
5 March–28 April	3	6	—	27	202	—	S.E. of Ypres (trench warfare).
29–30 April	—	—	—	1	15	—	Hill 60.
1 May	1	6	—	53	201	32	Hill 60 (1st gas attack).
2–4 May	—	—	—	3	12	—	Hill 60.
5 May	1	9	1	14	116	48	Hill 60 (2nd gas attack).
21 May–15 June	2	5	—	14	65	—	Hill 60 (trench warfare).
Total	14	42	5	224	1042	493	

Total Casualties (23rd August, 1914, to 15th June, 1915) 1820.

Note.—These figures have been compiled from the War Diary, and should be taken as approximately correct. It should be noted that the large number of other ranks reported " missing " on 13th and 22nd October, 1914, is due to the fact that the actions were fought on ground which at the close of the day was occupied by the enemy. A large number of these " missing " men were in fact killed or wounded.

The figures for 1st and 5th May, 1915, contain some 320 or more " gas " casualties.

APPENDIX E

Distances Marched Daily from Ors to Gagny

Date. 1914.	From.	To.	No. of miles.	
21 Aug.	Ors	Gommegnies	19	
22 Aug.	Gommegnies	Dour	15	
23 Aug.	Dour	Wasmes	8	Battle of Mons
24 Aug.	Wasmes	St. Vaast	15	Battle of Mons
25 Aug.	St. Vaast	Troisvilles	24	
26 Aug.	Troisvilles	Ponchaux	12	Battle of Le
27 Aug.	Ponchaux	Ollezy	23	Cateau
28 Aug.	Ollezy	Pontoise	20	
29 Aug.	Pontoise	Carlepont	4	
30 Aug.	Carlepont	Croutoy	12	
31 Aug.	Croutoy	Crepy-en-Valois	15	
1 Sept.	Crepy-en-Valois	Nanteuil	12	
2 Sept.	Nanteuil	Montge	10	
3 Sept.	Montge	Mont Pichet	15	
4 Sept.	No move.			
5 Sept.	Mont Pichet	Gagny	16	End of retreat

220 miles in 16 days, or 14 miles per diem.

Notes.—(*a*) Fifty per cent of the men in the ranks were Reservists.

(*b*) The weather throughout was intensely hot.

(*c*) Distances marched in the course of the actual operations of the battles of Mons and Le Cateau are not included.

MAP A. BATTLE OF MONS 23RD AND

CONDE. 9 Miles.

MONS — CONDE, CANAL.

ALL ATTEMPTS TO CROSS HELD UP TILL AFTER DARK 23rd AUG.

ALL ATTEMPTS TO CAPTURE CROSSING FAIL 23rd

14TH INF. BDE.
UNTIL 2 A.M. 24 AUG.

13TH INF. BDE.
ST. GHISLAIN UNTIL 2
THEN WITHDRAWN TO W

5TH DIV.

WAS

5TH GERMAN
DIV. 5 A.M. 24 AUG.

BOUSSU

5TH GERMAN
DIV. 5 A.M.
24. AUG.

HORNU

DORSE

VALENCIENNES 13 Miles

5TH GERMAN DIV. HELD

40.

Numerous
Slagheaps.

B. COY.

A.COY.
las 2
platoons

NORFOLKS   CHESHIRES
NIGHT 23/24 AUG. Railway Works.

Halte

Mine

Mine

Mine

60

BOIS DE
BOUSSU.

Champ - des - Sarts

Mine

Mine

Mine

80

5TH GERMAN
DIV. NIGHT
24/25 AUG.

PETIT
WASME

DORSETS.

GERMAN CORPS HALT FOR NIGHT

LINE OF RETIREMENT

6 P.M. 24 AUG.

DIA RE
CHESHIRES
NORFOLKS &
CHESHIRES.
(DIV. RES.)
24. AUG.

DOUR

100

WARQUIGNIES

BLAUGIES
2 Miles.

MILES 1   ¾   ½   ¼   0

CONTOUR INTERVAL - 20

TH AUGUST 1914.

CAPTURED BY 6TH GERMAN DIV. 5 P.M. 23RD AUG. MONS 2½ Miles.

MARIETTE
CAPTURED BY
3RD GERMAN
DIV. 5 P.M.
23RD AUG.

JEMAPPES

3RD DIV - WITH ITS
LEFT AT MARIETTE UNTIL
AFTERNOON 23 AUG. THEN
WITHDRAWN TO
FRAMERIES.

DIV.
8 P.M.
23 Aug.

QUAREGNON

REACHED BY GERMAN XII I CORPS

FLENU

6TH GERMAN DIV

Slagheap.

Station 8 P.M. 23RD AUG.

BEDFORDS

Station

Mine

24 AUG.

D. COY.

H.Q.

platoons
A COY.

Station

6TH GERMAN DIV.
ATTACKS. 8.30 A.M.
24 AUG.

Bn. H.Q.
2 plns A COY 8.30 A.M.
D Coy 24 AUG.
M.G. Sect
DORSETS

PATURAGES

6TH GERMAN

FRAMERIES.

Mine

LA BOUVERIE

DIV. NOON 24 AUG.

LEGEND

POSITIONS OF TROOPS

DORSETS. GREEN.
OTHER BRITISH TROOPS. RED
GERMANS. BLUE.
DIRECTION OF GERMAN
ATTACKS——→

SCALE.

2   3 MILES.

METRES.

MAP B. BATTLE OF LE CATEAU. 26TH AUG, 1914.

ATTACK OF GERMAN IV CORPS.

15 Inf. Bde

93 Inf. Regt

120

120

BEAUMONT

CAMBRAI: 10 M.

INCHY

9 Inf. Bde

TROISVILLES

2-18pr

B. Coy

2 platoons

½ C. Coy

½ C. Coy

Ld Suffolks

Dorsets

A. Coy

D. Coy.

Bde. Hd.

Norfolks

36 Fus. Regt

8th Div.

Bedfords

Bn. H.Q.

2 4-18 pr.

Cheshires

153 Inf. Regt.

7th Div.

13 Inf. Bde

66 Inf. Regt

26 Inf. Regt

13 Inf. Bde.

LE CATEAU.

14 Inf. Bde.

140

140

140

BERTRY

REUMONT

MAUROIS

HONNECHY

140

Advance of 27 Inf. Regt IV Corps 4 - 7 p.m.

Advance of Head of III Corps about 7 a.m.

SCALE: 3 INCHES TO 1·58 MILES.

MILES 1   ¾   ½   ¼   0   1   2 MILES

CONTOUR INTERVAL—20 METRES.

A. L. R
Apr. 1923.

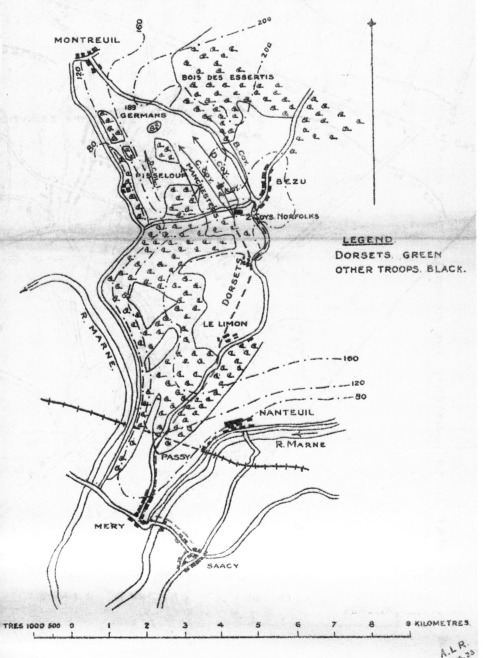

MAP. C. PASSAGE OF THE MARNE, 9TH SEPT. 1914.

MAP D. TO ILLUSTRATE THE FIGHTING ON THE R. AISNE. SEPT. 1914.

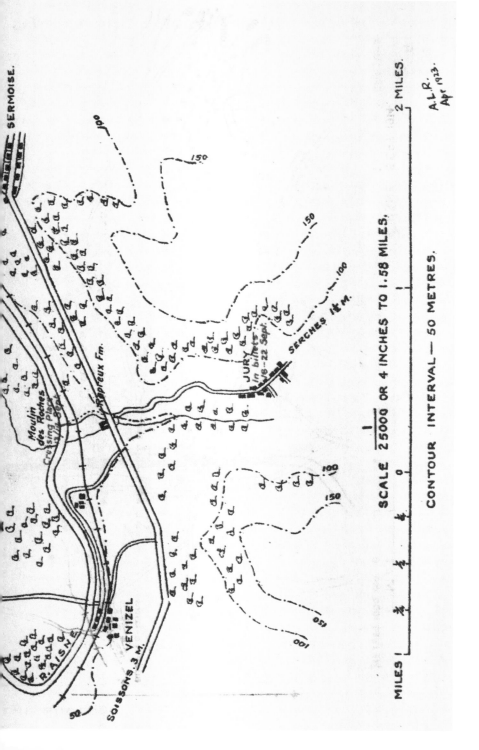

SERMOISE.

SOISSONS. 3 M.

R.AISNE

VENIZEL

Moulin des Roches
Crossing Place

Rispreux Fm.

JURY
in billets
18—22 Sept.

SERCHES 1¼ M.

100

150

150

100

100

150

100

150

50

SCALE $\frac{1}{25000}$ OR 4 INCHES TO 1.58 MILES.

CONTOUR INTERVAL — 50 METRES.

MILES 1   ¾   ½   ¼   0   1   2 MILES.

A.L.R.
Apr 1923.

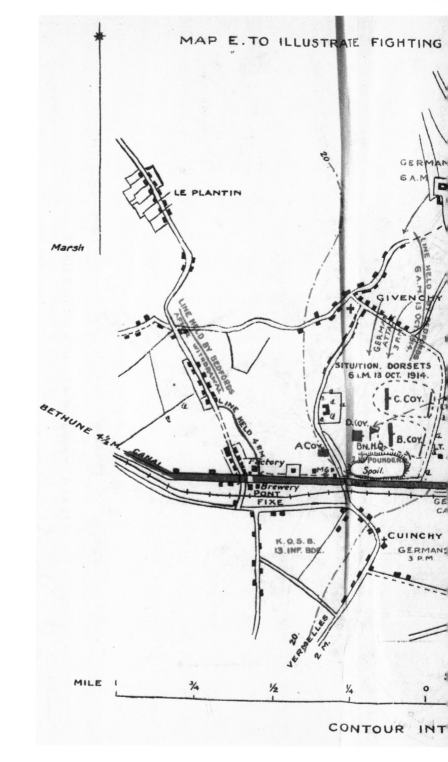

MAP E. TO ILLUSTRATE FIGHTING

LE PLANTIN

Marsh

GERMAN
6 A.M.

LINE HELD
6 A.M. 13 OCT.

GIVENCHY

LINE HELD BY BEDFORDS
AFTER WITHDRAWAL
LINE HELD 4 P.M.

GERMAN
ATTACK
3 P.M.

SITUATION. DORSETS
6 A.M. 13 OCT. 1914.

C. COY.

D. COY.

B. COY.

BETHUNE 4½ M.

CANAL

A. Coy.

BN. H.Q.

L.T.

Factory

MG.

60 POUNDER
Spoil.

Brewery
PONT
FIXE

GE
CA

K.O.S.B.
13. INF. BDE.

CUINCHY

GERMANS
3 P.M

VERMELLES
2 M.

20.

MILE 1   ¾   ½   ¼   0

CONTOUR INT

13TH OCTOBER 1914.

30

RUE D'OUVERT

CH^LLE ST. ROCH.

CANTELEUX

GERMAN ARTILLERY FIRE
10·5 C.M. HOW. 12 NOON.

GERMAN ADVANCE

ER'S
n

ER'S
n

GERMAN ADVANCE

CANAL   LA BASSÉE ¾ M.

S LINE
BANK

Brickstacks

GERMAN ADVANCE

LEGEND.
POSITION OF TROOPS.

DORSETS.	GREEN.
OTHER BRITISH TROOPS.	RED.
GERMANS	BLUE

LE.

1 MILE.

VAL - 10 METRES.

A.L.R.
AUG. 1922.

MAP OF GERMAN ATTACK ON VIOLAINES.
22ND OCT. 1914.

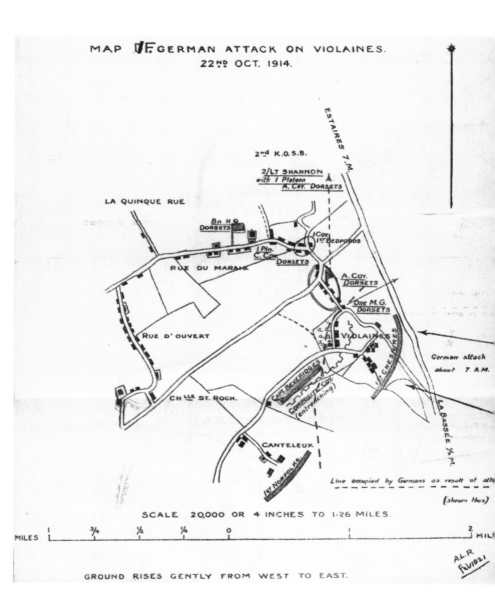

SCALE 20,000 OR 4 INCHES TO 1·26 MILES.

MILES ¾ ½ ¼ 0 1 2 MILES

GROUND RISES GENTLY FROM WEST TO EAST.

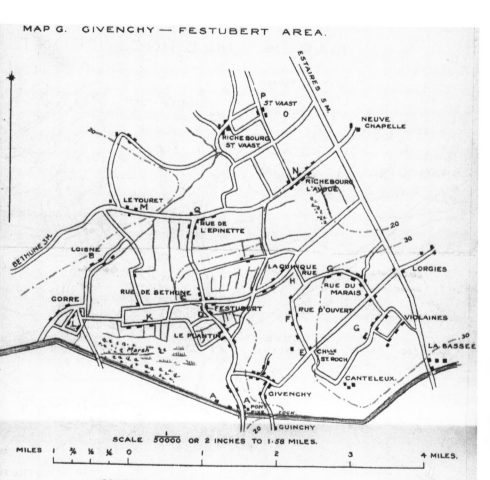

MAP G. GIVENCHY — FESTUBERT AREA.

ESTAIRES 5 M.

P ST VAAST O

NEUVE CHAPELLE

RICHEBOURG ST VAAST

N

RICHEBOURG L'AVOUÉ

LE TOURET M

Q

RUE DE L'EPINETTE

BETHUNE 5 M.

LOISNE B

LA QUINQUE RUE G

H

RUE DU MARAIS

LORGIES

RUE DE BETHUNE

O

FESTUBERT

RUE D'OUVERT

F

VIOLAINES

GORRE

L

K

G

LE PLANTIN

E

CH.LLE ST. ROCH

LA BASSÉE

Marsh

CANTELEUX.

A

A

GIVENCHY

PONT FIXE COCK.

GUINCHY

SCALE 50000 OR 2 INCHES TO 1·58 MILES.

MILES 1 ¾ ½ ¼ O   1   2   3   4 MILES.

CONTOUR INTERVAL – 10 METRES.

A.L.R.
JULY. 1922

LOCATION OF DORSETS 14 TH TO 30 TH OCT. 1914. IN

A 14th, 15th

B Night 15th/16th

C 16th, 17th, night 23rd/24th

D nights 16th/17th, 17th/18th, 22nd/23rd

E 18th, 19th

F Nights. 18th/19th, 19th/20th

G Nights. 20th/21st, 21st/22nd

H 22nd

K 23rd, 24th, 25th night 25th/26th

L 26th   M 27th   O 28th

N Night 27th/28th   Q 29th, 30th

P Night 27th/28th

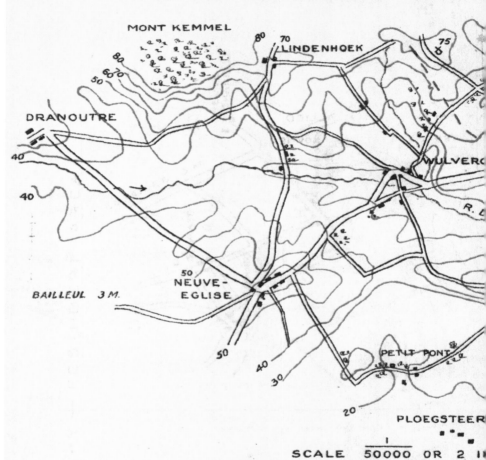

MAP H. MESSINES FRONT.

MONT KEMMEL

80 70
LINDENHOEK

75

80
60 70
50

DRANOUTRE

WULVERG

40

40

R. L

50
NEUVE-
EGLISE

BAILLEUL 3 M.

50

40
30
PETIT PONT

20

PLOEGSTEER

SCALE 50000 OR 2 I

MILES   1   ¾   ½   ¼   0   1

CONTOUR INTERVALS – 10 ME

APPROXIMATE ALLIED
FRONT LINE - *from* NOV. 1914.
shown thus _ _ _ _ _

WYTSCHAETE 2 M

50
40

MESSINES.
60
50
40
30

63
Chateau

ST YVES

Ploegsteert
Wood
20

LEGHEER

ES TO 1·58 MILES.

2   3 MILES.

S.

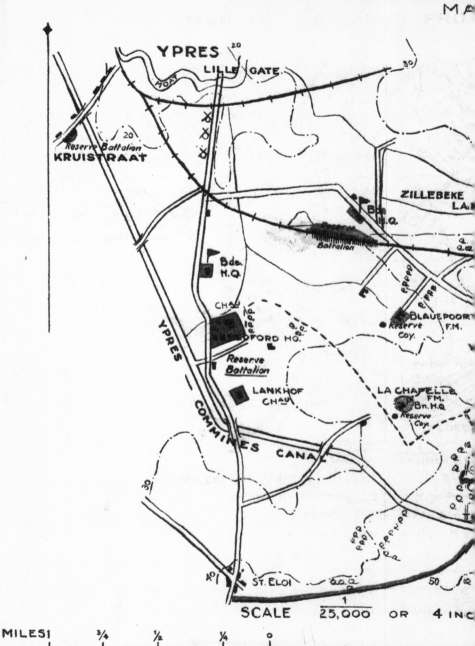

MAP K TO ILLUSTRATE

MA

SCALE 1/25,000 OR 4 INC

MILES 1   3/4   1/2   1/4   0

CONTOUR INTERVAL, 10 M

ZILLEBEKE

RANDEN-
LEN

Bn. H.Q.

Dump

HILL 60

ZWARTELEEN

Bn. H.Q.

Bn. H.Q.

International Trench

British Front Line (Trenches Numbered).

German Front Line (Approximate).

TO 1·58 MILES.

2 MILES

A. L. R
March 1923.

RES.

PLAN L. ROUGH DIAGRAM OF HILL 60 SECTOR (NOT TO SCALE)

SITUATION 7 P.M. 1ST MAY 1915.

Gas clouds

German bombing attacks

Gas clouds

German Sap-bing

Gas clouds

60

17 Bombing Centre Lancashire

42

C. Coy Dorsets

Bangalore

B. Coy. Dorsets

B. Coy. Dorsets

D. Coy. Dorsets

ZWARTELEEN (in ruins)

45   46   Belgians   43

47   Support

Shelters   42   Devons

A. Coy Dorsets

Track

38

39   41

disused

Communication Trench

YPRES – COMINES RAILWAY

Brick bridge   37   Norfolks

Dump

Ruined Farm.

Larch Wood

Shelters and dugouts   Devons

Hill   Devons and Dorsets

ZILLEBEKE ½ M.

SITUATION EVENING. 5TH MAY 1915.

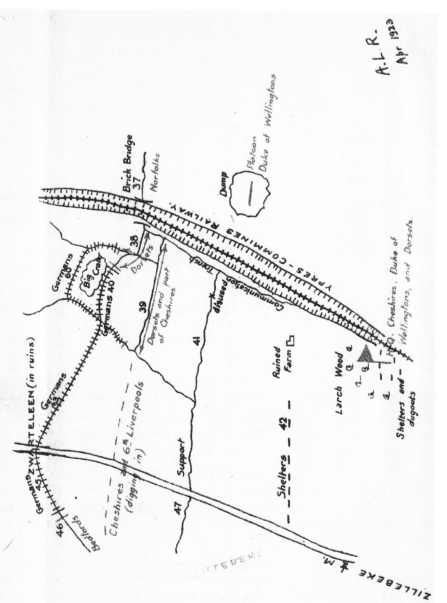

A.L.R.
Apr 1923

MAP X. TO ILLUSTRATE MARCHES
BETWEEN 21st AUGUST AND 5th OCT., 1914.

Route and halting places with date
shown in Gram.

● Me

● WASMES
DOUR
BLAUGIES
ATHIS
Franco-Belgian Frontier
St. VAAST
BAVAI
Preux ● Le Cheval blanc
GOMMEGNIES

Mormal Forest

● ENGLEFONTAINE

● CAUDRY
● LANDRECIES
LE CATEAU
CROISVILLES ● ORS
REUMONT

● MARETZ

● PONCHAUX
ESTREES

St. QUENTIN

R. Somme

HAM
OLLEZY
CUGNY

● GUISCARD

R. Oise

NOYON
PONTOISE
CARLEPONT

COMPEIGNE

ATTICHY
R. Aisne
MISSY
Campeigne Forest
CROUTOY
JURY
SERCHES
VERBERIE
FERME DE L'EPITAPHE
BETHISY
FRESNOY LA RIVIERE
NAMPTEUIL
NERY
ROQUEMONT
CORCY
LAUNOY
DUVY
St. REMY
CREPY-EN-VALOIS
BILLY
CHOUY
ORMOY-VILLERS
St. QUENTIN
NANTEUIL
CHEZY
GANDELU
GERMIGNY
DHUIZY
MONTREUIL
MONTGE
BEZU
TRILBARDOU
SAACY
MEAUX
Chateuesseuil
St. CYR
St. OUEN
ISLY
DOUE
R. Petit Morin
MONT PICHET
Gugnord
Le Chennis
MARCHES
BOISSY-LE-CHATEL
TRESMES
COULOMMIERS
VILLENEUVE
LAGELLE
MONTCERF
● TOURNAN

● GAGNY

SCALE 500000 OR 1 INCH TO 7·97 MILES

MILES 10   8   6   4   2   0   10   20   30 MILES

TELEGRAMS,
DOLPHIN, PLYMOUTH.
TELEPHONE Nº 124.

ROYAL WESTERN YACHT CLUB OF ENGLAND,
PLYMOUTH.

4ᵗʰ Aug 1923

My dear Major.

I am sending you herewith a copy of the short account of the early part of the war, the manuscript of which you were good enough to read a year or so ago. I fear it isn't up to much, but merely an effort to produce some record of those early days of the great war.

My kind regards to Mrs Ridley & yourself.

Yours very sincerely

AJ Ransome

Lightning Source UK Ltd.
Milton Keynes UK
UKOW06f0109170616

276431UK00013B/91/P